Noah

Noah helps pairs of animals enter the ark. Detail from a 13th century Byzantine mosaic.

Money at its Best: Millionaires of the Bible

Abraham and Sarah
Daniel
David
Esther
Jacob
Job

Joseph
Moses
Noah
Samson
Solomon
Wealth in Biblical Times

MONEY at its BEST

Noah

Stephen B. Woodruff

Mason Crest Publishers
Philadelphia

Produced by OTTN Publishing.
Cover design © 2008 TLC Graphics, www.TLCGraphics.com.

Mason Crest Publishers
370 Reed Road, Suite 302
Broomall PA 19008
www.masoncrest.com

Copyright © 2009 by Mason Crest Publishers. All rights reserved.
Printed and bound in The United States of America.

First printing

1 3 5 7 9 8 6 4 2

Library of Congress Cataloging-in-Publication Data

  Woodruff, Stephen B.
   Noah / Stephen B. Woodruff.
     p. cm. — (Millionaires of the Bible)
   Includes bibliographical references (p.   ) and index.
   ISBN 978-1-4222-0474-0 (alk. paper)
   ISBN 978-1-4222-0849-6 (pbk. : alk. paper)
  1. Noah (Biblical figure) I. Title.
  BS580.N6W66 2008
  222'.11092—dc22
                                            2008011682

Publisher's Note: The Web sites listed in this book were active at the time of publication. The publisher is not responsible for Web sites that have changed their address or discontinued operation since the date of publication. The publisher reviews and updates the Web sites each time the book is reprinted.

Table of Contents

Noah and His Wealth	6
Introduction: Wealth and Faith	7
1. The Noah Controversy	11
2. Creation in Crisis	23
3. The Coming Disaster	38
4. The End of the World	50
5. A Saving Memory	61
6. New Creation and Future Blessings	70
7. Noah of the Vineyard	80
8. Understanding Noah Today	87
Notes	98
Glossary	102
Further Reading	104
Internet Resources	105
Index	107
Illustration Credits	111
About the Author	112

Noah and His Wealth

- Noah's wealth is not specifically discussed in the Bible. However, he was a man who walked with God, and God looked favorably on Noah (Genesis 6). Noah had spiritual wealth—it was not tangible, but it was worth more than riches could ever buy, because his faith saved his life. After the Flood, God blessed Noah and his family with material wealth.

- When Noah and his family left the ark, God made a covenant with Noah and blessed him, saying "Be fruitful and increase in number and fill the earth. . . . I now give you everything" (Genesis 9:1-3). As steward of God's new creation, Noah was the richest man on earth.

- According to the Bible and Jewish legends, Noah owned a vineyard where he produced wine. This is a sign of material wealth, because wine was highly prized in biblical times.

- Noah was the first post-Flood Patriarch of the Jewish faith. His sons established new cities in new lands, following God's command to re-populate the earth. "From these the nations spread out over the earth after the flood" (Genesis 10:32).

- Today, no one knows how prosperous Noah was. In the words of the New Testament scripture, "store up for yourselves treasures in heaven, where moth and rust do not destroy" (Matthew 6:20). Noah's true wealth lay in his faith and his relationship with God.

Introduction: Wealth and Faith

Many people believe strongly that great personal wealth is incompatible with deep religious belief—that like oil and water, the two cannot be mixed. Christians, in particular, often feel this way, recollecting Jesus Christ's own teachings on wealth. "Do not store up for yourselves treasures on earth, where moth and rust destroy, and where thieves break in and steal," Jesus cautions during the Sermon on the Mount (Matthew 6:19). In Luke 18:25, he declares, "It is easier for a camel to go through the eye of a needle than for a rich man to enter the kingdom of God"—a sentiment repeated elsewhere in the Gospels.

Yet in Judeo-Christian culture there is a long-standing tradition of material wealth as the manifestation of God's blessing. This tradition is amply reflected in the books of the Hebrew Bible (or as Christians know them, the Old Testament). Genesis 13:2 says that the patriarch Abram (Abraham) "had become very wealthy in livestock and in silver and gold"; the Bible makes it clear that this prosperity is a gift from God. Other figures whose lives are chronicled in

Genesis—including Isaac, Jacob, Joseph, Noah, and Job—are described as both wealthy and righteous. The book of Deuteronomy expresses God's promise of prosperity for those who obey his commandments:

> If you fully obey the Lord your God and carefully follow all his commands I give you today, the Lord your God will set you high above all the nations on earth. . . . The Lord will grant you abundant prosperity—in the fruit of your womb, the young of your livestock and the crops of your ground—in the land he swore to your forefathers to give you. (Deuteronomy 28:1, 11)

A key requirement for this prosperity, however, is that God's blessings must be used to help others. Deuteronomy 15:10–11 says, "Give generously . . . and do so without a grudging heart; then because of this the Lord your God will bless you in all your work and in everything you put your hand to." The book of Proverbs—written during the time of Solomon, one of history's wealthiest rulers—similarly presents wealth as a desirable blessing that can be obtained through hard work, wisdom, and following God's laws. Proverbs 14:31 promises, "The faithless will be fully repaid for their ways, and the good man rewarded for his."

Numerous stories and folktales show the generosity of the patriarchs. According to Jewish legend, Job owned an inn at a crossroads, where he allowed travelers to eat and drink at no cost. When they offered to pay, he instead told them about God, explaining that he was simply a steward of the wealth that God had given to him and urging them to worship God, obey God's commands, and receive their own blessings. A story about Abraham says that when he moved his flocks from one field to another, he would muzzle the animals so that they would not graze on a neighbor's property.

After the death of Solomon, however, the kingdom of Israel

was divided and the people fell away from the commandments God had mandated. The later writings of the prophets, who are attempting to correct misbehavior, specifically address unethical acts committed to gain wealth. "You trample on the poor," complained the prophet Amos. "You oppress the righteous and take bribes and you deprive the poor of justice in the courts" (Amos 5:11, 12). The prophet Isaiah insists, "Learn to do right! Seek justice, encourage the oppressed. . . . If you are willing and obedient, you will eat the best from the land; but if you resist and rebel, you will be devoured by the sword" (Isaiah 1:17, 19–20).

Viewed in this light, the teachings of Jesus take on new meaning. Jesus does not condemn wealth; he condemns those who would allow the pursuit of wealth to come ahead of the proper relationship with God: "No one can serve two masters. . . . You cannot serve both God and money" (Matthew 6:24).

Today, nearly everyone living in the Western world could be considered materially wealthier than the people of the Bible, who had no running water or electricity, lived in tents, walked when traveling long distances, and wore clothing handmade from animal skins. But we also live in an age when tabloid newspapers and trashy television programs avidly follow the misadventures of spoiled and selfish millionaire athletes and entertainers. In the mainstream news outlets, it is common to read or hear reports of corporate greed and malfeasance, or of corrupt politicians enriching themselves at the expense of their constituents. Often, the responsibility of the wealthy to those members of the community who are not as successful seems to have been forgotten.

The purpose of the series MONEY AT ITS BEST: MILLIONAIRES OF THE BIBLE is to examine the lives of key figures from biblical history, showing how these people used their wealth or their powerful and privileged positions in order to make a difference in the lives of others.

This Victorian-era stained glass window from a church in Fringford, England, depicts Noah holding a model of the ark.

1

THE NOAH CONTROVERSY

Thunder and lightning raged across the sky. The creaking wooden vessel rode the waves, dipping and rolling, floating higher than the highest mountains. Inside huddled an old man and his family. The stagnant air was thick with the scent and sound of animal life. Outside, death raged across the earth; the churning waters overwhelmed every living thing. The only safety was in the floating sanctuary. Despite pitch sealing the cracks between the boards, the gopher-wood vessel leaked readily, its lower deck collecting water. Death and drowning might be easier than facing the awful reality outside. If only the rain would cease!

The tale of Noah is one of the world's best-known stories. It is thousands of years old, and can be found in the sacred scriptures of Judaism, Christianity, and Islam. Noah's story was preserved and carried forward by oral tradition, told and retold through many generations.

In the Biblical story God destroyed an evil world but saved Noah, his family, and the animals, two by two. God used them to repopulate the earth and start over again. The people of all three monotheistic faiths hold Noah in high regard. "By faith Noah, being warned by God concerning events as yet unseen, took heed and constructed an ark for the saving of his household," wrote the Apostle Paul in the first century. "By this he condemned the world and became an heir of the righteousness which comes by faith" (Hebrews 11:7). Like other figures whose stories are told in the scriptures, Noah had a special relationship to God because he lived a righteous, faithful life.

Noah is a well-known figure—even people who are not religious can identify him. He and his voyage on an ark full of animals are the subject of paintings and sculptures in the great museums of the world. Children in parochial schools sing songs recalling Noah and his ark. Many people feel a bond to Noah. He is everyone's kinsman, and, according to the Bible, he is the forefather of all people alive today.

The story of Noah and his ark fascinates both children and adults.

WHO WAS NOAH?

In the first book of the Hebrew Bible, which essentially corresponds to the Christian Old Testament, Noah is described as the grandson of Methuselah and the son of Lamech, born ten generations after God's creation of the first man and woman, Adam and Eve. Unfortunately, in Noah's lifetime humans have succumbed to evil, and refuse to follow the teachings of God. However, like his great-grandfather Enoch before him, Noah is said to "walk with the Lord."

As the only right-living man, Noah and his family are chosen to continue the human line after God's Flood destroys the world. Noah becomes a second Adam, father of the human race, and leads the Flood survivors into a new creation, a new relationship with God.

Throughout the story, little is mentioned about Noah's material possessions other than the ark that he built. His spiritual wealth and inner goodness set him apart from a seriously damaged creation, a world headed for disaster. Noah's name itself is meaningful, translated as "rest, quiet, comfort." Noah's name predicts his future importance. "[Lamech] named him Noah and said, "He will comfort us in the labor and painful toil of our hands caused by the ground the LORD has cursed." (Genesis

---

Noah is considered an important figure in the traditions of three major world religions: Judaism, Christianity, and Islam. Each of these religions developed in the region today known as the Middle East. While the religions have many differences, they all share a belief that there is only one God, and that He is involved in human affairs.

5:29–30). Methuselah called him Noah, but Lamech and others called him Menahem, which means "comforter," the legends say.

Some scholars suggest Noah comforted the world because, after the Flood, he tilled the soil, planted a vineyard, and invented wine, a comforting drink. Wine was prized in ancient times, the drink made to "cheer gods and men" (Judges 9:13b). Other legends told by Jewish rabbis associate Noah's comforting the world with inventions that simplified earthly labor: the plow, scythe, hoe, and other tools of cultivation. Before him, say these legends, there were no tools; men worked the land with their hands. It is not clear whether Noah invented these tools before or after the Flood. Some traditions have suggested that before the Flood, Noah was a farmer, and that he developed these tools to make hard labor easier.

If we follow the biblical timetable, Noah lived in the ancient past, as far removed from the patriarch Abraham as we in this century are from the time of Jesus Christ. Having a vineyard in those times, making wine, may suggest that Noah was a man of means. Certainly these would have been of value. But little is known about Noah's first 600 years of life, except that he followed in the footsteps of Enoch and Methuselah. He carried out their appointed task: preaching a message to save the world from its evil ways. If he was involved in a trade of some kind, if he raised animals, or if he was a farmer, we can only guess.

In the Qur'an, the holy scriptures of Islam, Noah is numbered with the prophets and with some of the faith's greatest teachers: "Truly Allah chose Adam and Noah and the descendants of Abraham and the descendants of Amran above the nations. . . . Surely we have revealed to thee as we revealed to Noah and prophets after him, and we revealed to Abraham and Ishmael and Isaac and Jacob and the tribes, and Jesus and Job and Jonah and Aaron and Solomon" (Qur'an 3:33; 4:163).

In the Christian tradition, Noah is a forerunner of Jesus. The Apostle Peter writes that after Jesus' crucifixion and death, the messiah goes to preach to the spirits in

In Judeo-Christian and Muslim traditions, Noah stands in a line of faithful men whose lives illustrated righteousness and found favor with God. These statues at Cologne Cathedral, Germany, depict Moses, David, Elijah, Noah, and John the Baptist.

the world of the dead. His hearers include "ones who formerly did not obey when God's patience waited in the days of Noah, during the building of the ark, in which a few . . . persons were saved through water" (1 Peter 3:18–22). The waters of baptism are equated with the waters of the Flood. The Flood water cleansed the earth in the same way Christians believe baptism cleanses and prepares souls for a relationship with God.

The Controversy About Noah

Noah's story is controversial among biblical scholars. The controversy surrounding the Noah story is not so much with Noah himself, but with the nature of biblical interpretation. Noah means different things to different people.

Nonreligious people view the Noah story as a folktale, as they do all of scripture. They point out the unbelievable aspects of the story: a worldwide flood (which they believe is not supported by any scientific or archaeological evidence); the seeming impossibility of thousands of pairs of living things living together on a large, wooden boat; the idea that one elderly couple and their three married sons could populate the earth. To them, Noah is a fictional character in a fairy tale.

Religious people approach the Flood story in different ways. A scholar writes:

> The first eleven chapters of Genesis are among the most important in Scripture . . . the best known (in a stereotyped way). And they are frequently the most misunderstood. . . . A faithful understanding of these materials requires that interpreters be clear about the nature of the material presented and the relationship it has to the remainder of Scripture.

A LITERAL INTERPRETATION

Some people believe scripture—all scripture—is literally true. They claim the Bible is historically accurate and divinely inspired—error free, because it was written by God. Even non-religious writers in ancient times approached Noah and the Flood from this vantage point. They believed the ark's landing spot had been discovered and its remains visible. For example, the first century Jewish historian Flavius Josephus wrote, "In a district called Carra . . . the remains of the ark in which report has it that Noah was saved from the flood . . . to this day are shown to those who are curious to see them." Theophilus, the second-century bishop of Antioch, wrote, "The remains of the ark are to be seen in the Arabian mountains to this day."

Many of these ancient "sightings" occurred in different places on many mountains. Muslims even identified a resting place for the ark in the Arabian Desert. The ancients had no way to verify the sightings or the evidence, if it existed. They had the legend itself, as it had been told to them. They accepted the story as true. The ancient writers wrote at least 4,000 years after Noah's Flood, according to biblical calculations. Facts can easily be lost or altered in such a time span. To date, no hard evidence has verified their sightings.

There are modern believers who also have a literal understanding of Noah and the Flood. They, like their ancient counterparts, believe the story happened as reported in Genesis. Their evidence is the unerring Bible itself. They have calculated the date of the moment of Creation and have computed the date of the Flood as well. They believe the story of Noah chronicles how an angry God saved one man and his family, then wiped the world clean of sin. For them, the story illustrates the value of faith and of being righteous. It teaches how God hates sin, and shows how he rewards those who do right in his eyes.

A Scholarly Interpretation

On the other hand, many scholars believe the story of Noah and the Flood is not literal history. But they do believe it is a story vital to understanding the faith of the ancient people who included it in their sacred scriptures. These scholars analyze the Biblical text and other ancient writings about Noah using different approaches. Each method involves study in the original languages, unveiling the many shades of meaning in the words. Scholars note different styles of narrative. They examine the text in an attempt to determine whether a passage was written by a single author or if it seems to be a composite piece assembled by an ancient editor. Changes in the style of writing or in the vocabulary may indicate the passage was authored by more than one person. The way God is named, for example, can indicate more than one author in a passage. (For further explanation of textual analysis, see "The Documentary Hypothesis," page 19.)

In addition, modern scholars use archaeological discoveries to weigh the truth of scriptural material. Over the past two centuries, archaeology has supported many of the stories and details found in scripture: the structure and location of cities and villages, the seminomadic lifestyle of the people, and the social customs of the day.

The story of Joseph being sold into slavery by his brothers, told in the book of Genesis, is one such example of how the scriptural stories are supported by modern discoveries. One ancient text describes how a man sold his friend to a passing caravan on the way to Egypt, just as Joseph was sold. A papyrus scroll dated to around 1800 B.C.E. lists Semitic peoples enslaved in Egypt, which

The Documentary Hypothesis

According to a longstanding tradition among Christians and Jews, Moses is the author of Genesis. However, contemporary scholars generally agree that Genesis is the work of four distinct authors or groups of authors who compiled and edited material from different locations and sources over a period of centuries.

During the late 19th century, a theory of biblical authorship called the Documentary Hypothesis was formulated. Over the years there have been numerous variations on this theory. In its simplest form, the Documentary Hypothesis says that the main blocks of stories in the books of Genesis and Exodus—including the story of Noah—are the oldest material. They are attributed to two anonymous authors, known as J and E. The initials come from the names for God that each author uses in the narrative —J for "Yahweh" (in German, "Jahweh") and E for "Elohim." Scholars believe these two sets of stories were written down between 950 and 800 B.C.E., although they probably existed in oral form much earlier than that.

Around 600 B.C.E., new material concerned with religious or legal matters—such as the covenant between God and Abraham in Genesis 17, along with genealogical information—was added. This material is believed to have been the work of a priest or group of priests, and is labeled P.

The first five books of the Bible (referred to by Jews as the Torah) were placed in their final form around 400 B.C.E. by a group of editors, who blended the J, E, and P strands together and added new material. The addition is labeled R, after the group of redactors who concentrated on reworking and polishing the text.

Over the past two centuries the Biblical text has been the subject of intense scholarly scrutiny. This theory offers an understanding of how the book of Genesis might have been composed. However, there are still numerous points of disagreement among scholars, and many of them may be impossible to ever resolve.

seems to support the description of the enslaved Hebrews in the book of Exodus.

To date, however, archaeologists have not found evidence of a man named Noah (except in scripture) or of a flood of worldwide proportion (except in ancient legends).

Archaeologists working in the Middle East have identified past floods where one city was struck but others nearby were spared. Sometimes a section of a city shows flood deposits, while other locations in the same city show none. Twentieth-century excavations explored the ancient Mesopotamian cities of Ur, Kish, Shuruppak, Ninevah, and others. All showed deposits of sediment thick enough to have been caused by settling sediments during a flood. But closer examination and dating revealed that the time periods did not match each other; the sediments were found to have been left by river flooding and wind deposits. The ancient world contains flood evidence, but so far, not evidence of the Flood of Noah.

The Hebrews were not the only culture of the Middle East with a story about a Great Flood. Sumerians, Assyrians, and Babylonians all had separate but similar Flood accounts. They may be related to the story of Noah, though these stories have different heroes, differing causes for the Flood, and different outcomes for the hero.

FINDING NOAH'S VALUE TODAY

Scholars find different ways of probing old stories, especially those in the first 11 chapters of Genesis, the primeval history. Scholars believe "the [primeval histories] are symbolic, mythical accounts . . . they do not record events which can be validated by contemporary evidence."

Modern biblical scholars seek to learn more about the time when documents containing the story of Noah's Flood were created. Scholars attempt to identify the origi-

After being saved from the Flood, Noah's first instinct was to give thanks to God. Genesis 8:20–21 says, "Then Noah built an altar to the Lord and, taking some of all the clean animals and clean birds, he sacrificed burnt offerings on it. The LORD smelled the pleasing aroma and said in his heart: 'Never again will I curse the ground because of man, even though every inclination of his heart is evil from childhood. And never again will I destroy all living creatures, as I have done.'"

nal audience. They try to interpret the theological purposes of the writer or editor. The Noah story for them does not have significance as a historical event. What matters to them is the message this story brought about God to the original hearers. Only then, in their view, can the story of Noah speak to modern hearers.

These scholars believe the primeval stories of Genesis 1–11 do not conflict with science and modern discoveries. But many people reject them because they do not report the history of the beginning of the world as science has. Disbelievers state the scientific impossibility of the story. If one cannot believe in Noah as the story is presented, then how does one know what to believe? The Noah story is sometimes used to reject religion altogether.

When viewed with modern scientific eyes, many Bible stories seem impossible. But some would argue that using the Bible as a science text has resulted in the confusion; the intent of the early chapters of Genesis had another purpose. The intent of the material (especially the primeval history) is to reveal truth in poetic form. The historical-sounding events matter less than the deeper meaning behind the story.

The value of the story of Noah exists on many levels. What the stories say about God, and why this ancient tale is still treasured today, thousands of years since it was first told, is the subject of this book.

Another Flood Story

The best-known and most complete alternate version of the Flood is the Gilgamesh epic, found on the 11th stone tablet discovered in the library of Ashurbanipal (669–627 B.C.E.). It concerns the hero Utnapishtim, who receives a warning of impending disaster. He builds a boat, saving his family, other humans, and animals. It is such a frightening deluge that even the gods who caused it are afraid. They run back to heaven, crying, and crouch behind a wall. Utnapishtim's reward for his saving action was immortality.

The story of Gilgamesh parallels the Noah account in many ways—enough to convince many modern scholars that a common source story, or perhaps an actual flood that occurred in the Middle East at some time, preceded them.

Creation in Crisis

What was wrong with creation? How bad could creation have become that the only thing God could do was destroy it all and start again? Before telling the story of Noah's life, the sad state of creation must be described. The story of Noah must be placed in a biblical context to clarify why God decided to destroy his entire creation except for one man, his family, and a representative population of animals.

In the Bible, the Noah story begins near the end of the primeval history, the accounts of God's dealings with creation in the generations after Adam and Eve.

The Time Before Noah: What Went Wrong?

In the generations before Noah's birth, humans corrupted the earth so completely that a new beginning is necessary. Creation is moving in a direction that God had not intended, even though God has been clear to his people. They must continue to be connected and accountable to the Creator. Creation and its creatures need to know their place. A prominent biblical scholar writes:

> The creator has a purpose and a will for creation. The creation exists only because of that will. The creator continues to address the creation, calling it to faithful response and glad obedience to his will. The creation has not been turned loose on its own. It has not been abandoned. Nor has it been given free rein . . . the creator loves and respects the creation. . . . [Its] freedom is taken seriously.

God has created the world and everything in it, including Adam and Eve, then admires what he has done. "And God saw everything that he had made, and behold, it was very good" (Genesis 1:31). God releases his newly created humans into a paradise with the command to "be fruitful and multiply" and rule the earth (Genesis 1:28b). However, with their almost limitless freedom Adam and Eve are given one simple command to follow: "Of the tree

---

Jewish legends are tales that have been told over the centuries but that do not come directly from the Tanakh, or Jewish Bible. They are often derived from the Talmud (an authoritative collection of Jewish laws and legal decisions, along with commentary) and the Midrash (stories that expand on Bible incidents, to illustrate legal or moral principles). Rabbis often used the Midrash to fill in gaps in the Torah (the first five books of the Tanakh). Collectively, these stories are also called *Haggadah*, the Hebrew word for legends of the Bible.

Stained glass window depicting the fall of creation, as described in the third chapter of Genesis: "When the woman saw that the fruit of the tree was good for food and pleasing to the eye, and also desirable for gaining wisdom, she took some and ate it. She also gave some to her husband, who was with her, and he ate it. Then the eyes of both of them were opened, and they realized they were naked; so they sewed fig leaves together and made coverings for themselves. . . ."

"And the Lord God said, 'The man has now become like one of us, knowing good and evil. He must not be allowed to reach out his hand and take also from the tree of life and eat, and live forever.' So the Lord God banished him from the Garden of Eden to work the ground from which he had been taken" (Genesis 3:6–7, 22–23).

of the knowledge of good and evil you shall not eat" (Genesis 2:17).

It does not take long for things to go wrong. Adam and Eve are told by a serpent, "When you eat of [the fruit of the tree] your eyes will be opened, and you will be like God" (Genesis 3:5). Of course, they eat. Then creation begins a downward spiral ending in a sickening splash: the destruction of the world by flood.

In the Midrash—Jewish stories and legends that expand on Biblical stories—the fall of Adam is considered a story about the consequences of freedom. Humans have an awful, terrifying freedom to choose good or evil. And humans can easily go either way. Unfortunately, throughout the early chapters of Genesis, humanity tends to follow the second impulse time and time again. For example, Adam and Eve's son, Cain, kills his brother Abel. For this horrible crime, Cain is driven away from his parents.

The descendants of Cain (known as Cainites) will become one of two branches of humanity; the other is descended from Cain's younger brother, Seth. Cain and his descendants are credited with building cities, but also with erecting temples to idols. They invent music, but

Cain kills his brother, Abel, as described in Genesis 4:8. Painting by the famed Renaissance artist Titian, circa 1570.

Tubal-Cain, a son of Lamech, learns how to work iron and copper to fashion weapons of war. According to the Midrash, skill in metallurgy was exhibiting "knowledge of the gods" and was therefore off-limits to humans.

During the generations that follow, the Cainites blend into the growing mass of humanity on earth. Their evil ways further distance them from God: lewd behavior, faithless marriages, warlike ways, and engagement in robberies. One of Cain's descendants, a man named Lamech (not the father of Noah), even brags about killing a man out of vengeance, rather than feeling sorry for what he has done.

The Bible account stops following the Cainites' progress and turns its attention to the descendants of Seth, the immediate ancestors of Noah.

AFTER ADAM AND EVE

Seth, the third son of Adam and Eve, begins the lineage leading to Noah. In chapter 5, the Genesis account tells no story at all, but lists the generations extending from Seth, Adam and Eve's good son: Seth, Enosh, Kenan, Mahalalel, Jared, Enoch, Methuselah, Lamech, and Noah (Genesis 5:1–28). Seth's descendants live righteous lives in a world that continues to be corrupt, violent, and full of evil.

Conditions worsen in the time of Enosh, son of Seth. According to Jewish legends, people of this generation worship idols, gathering gold, silver, gems, and pearls to construct them. Worse, after God expels Adam and Eve from the Garden of Eden, the Shekinah, God's holy presence, remains at the garden gate. The angels descend to the Shekinah to receive instructions for their holy missions. But instead of going about their business, they linger and mingle with the descendants of Adam. These angels teach the people magic arts, and humans become like the angels, a little too like God himself. The fallen humans use their new knowledge to take control of the heavenly spheres, the sun, the moon, and the stars; they have powers far beyond those intended for mortal beings. They possess beautiful things.

God has lost control over his creatures; the world has gone hopelessly wrong. Jewish Midrash speculates that unbounded affluence—great wealth—caused humans to fall. They had too much free time on their hands—time to get themselves into trouble.

THE FALL OF THE ANGELS

In the time of Jared, Genesis reports that angels descend to earth, attracted to the beautiful daughters of men. They marry, producing children who are gigantic in stature—superhumans—sometimes known as the "men of renown" (Genesis 6:4). The Bible calls them Nephilim, and next to them, men "seemed . . . like grasshoppers [in size]" (Numbers 13:33).

When angels descended to earth, they lost their transcendental qualities and acquired earthly bodies. Their offspring were these giants, known for both their strength and their sinfulness. The name *Nephilim* means "bringing the world to its fall, they themselves fell." This is an unnatural condition, the blending of heavenly and earthly creatures. God did not intend this. Creation's crash continues.

Not only do the angels father children by the daughters of men, they teach them charms and the secrets of plants. They teach them to make metal weapons and to paint their faces and eyes. They impart knowledge reserved for God and his heavenly court. Gaining the knowledge of the gods makes people like God, at least in their own eyes. But God cannot tolerate this condition for long.

CRISIS IN CREATION

In these generations before Noah, creation is out of control. The boundary between heaven and earth has been shattered. Modern scholar David Patterson writes, "Creation is undermined by [sin;] it arises when we lose the capacity for making distinctions between what is above and what is below, as, for example, when we take ourselves to be as God." This corruption affects not only the humans, but also the earth, the creation, itself. A kabbalistic tale tells of Rabbi Yitzchak asking Rabbi Shimon how the earth can be considered corrupt when it is humans who are corrupt in their hearts and minds. Rabbi Shimon responds:

> Because all of humanity is made of the earth. Indeed, the dust from which God created man was gathered from the four corners of the earth. As we treat one another, so we treat the earth that comes from the hand of God. When one human being betrays another, he betrays all of God's creation.

Creation has stopped listening, and, according to the Old Testament scholar and author Walter Brueggemann, "when creation does not listen, it cannot respond as God's creation . . . God's call is sovereign, but unheeded." As the scriptural and apocryphal accounts draw nearer to the time of Noah, God continues to call. There is a hope that humans will hear. God desires to be in relationship with His creation. But creation is too busy going its own way.

ENOCH

Throughout this evil time, God remained active in the lives of the faithful descendents of Seth, namely Enoch and his son, Methuselah. While angels fell and heavenly beings mingled with and corrupted the world, Enoch apparently lived a holy life. The Biblical account of Enoch's life is only four sentences long:

> When Enoch had lived 65 years, he became the father of Methuselah. And after he became the father of Methuselah, Enoch walked with God 300 years and had other sons and daughters. Altogether, Enoch lived 365 years. Enoch walked with God; then he was no more, because God took him away (Genesis 5:21–24).

Jewish legends, however, fleshed out the story of Enoch, describing how God worked through this righteous man in an effort to bring creation back to the proper path. According to one legend, God sends Enoch to the renegade angels to proclaim their doom. They are terror-struck and plead with Enoch to talk with God on their behalf.

Enoch agrees, and in a vision, he goes to heaven and approaches God. He receives a difficult command. God orders him to go back to the rebellious angels and ask them how they could have given up all the glories of heaven to corrupt their lives. How could they lower themselves to take human women as wives, ending their unique relationship with God? Enoch does as God commands, but, ultimately, the fallen angels refuse to change their ways.

In another story, God tells Enoch to go out among men and teach them how they should be living their lives. Enoch sends out messengers, who invite the people to approach Enoch and learn from him. Vast numbers of people come—kings and princes included—and his teaching is so effective that peace reigns for 243 years.

After this, Enoch withdraws from society little by little, appearing to others only occasionally and spending most of his time in contemplation. The legends describe how Enoch visits heaven in dreams, achieving a special relationship with God and even receiving a new name, Metatron. The effect of Enoch's relationship with God is physically apparent: Each time he appears to the people, his countenance is more awe-inspiring and majestic. When people see him, they fall on their faces and cry out.

Enoch speaks with an angel. Detail from an European altar decoration, circa 1181.

Eventually, Enoch is carried to heaven in a fiery chariot—a detail similar to the Biblical description of the Prophet Elijah's ascent to heaven.

"The sinfulness of men was the reason why Enoch was translated to heaven," wrote the great Hebrew scholar Louis Ginzberg in his collection of Jewish folklore, *Legends of the Jews*. "When the generation of the deluge [Flood] transgressed, and spoke to God, saying, 'Depart from us, for we do not desire to know thy ways,' Enoch was carried to heaven,to serve there as a witness that God was not a cruel God in spite of the destruction decreed upon all living things on earth."

METHUSELAH AND LAMECH

After Enoch is carried to heaven, Methuselah, his son, becomes ruler of the earth. Methuselah is known for being the longest-lived man in the Bible. Genesis 5:25–27 reports that Methuselah was 187 years old when he became the father of Lamech, and that he lived for another 782 years and had other sons and daughters.

Again, various Jewish legends add details about the long life of Methuselah. Ginzberg wrote, "[Methuselah] walked in the footsteps of his father, teaching truth, knowledge, and fear of God to the children of men all his life, and deviating from the path . . . neither to the right nor the left."

The Talmud, an extensive collection of commentary on the Bible by Jewish rabbis that also includes history and interpretation of religious laws, reports that despite Methuselah's efforts, the people "grew regardless of his teachings. They disregarded the personal rights of one another, and rebelled against the commands of God."

God attempts to turn them back, even creating havoc in agriculture. According to one legend, God causes everything planted to spring up as thorns and thistles, but the people do not repent. God decides he must destroy the earth. About this time, Noah, son of Lamech, is born.

Noah's Birth

Ancient Jewish writings, such as the book of Enoch, provide details about the birth of Noah that is not included in the Genesis account. In Genesis, Lamech says, "Out of the ground which the Lord has cursed this one shall bring us relief from our work and from the toil of our hands" (Genesis 5:29). But in the legends of the Jews, we learn that the baby Noah "was white as snow and red as a blooming rose, and the hair of his head and his long locks were white as wool, and his eyes like the rays of the sun . . . and he opened his mouth and praised the Lord of righteousness."

Lamech is afraid of the baby Noah, for obvious reasons. He runs to Methuselah for advice, fearful that this child might be a child of angels. He begs Methuselah to search for Enoch and learn the truth. Methuselah agrees, goes to the ends of the earth, and calls out to Enoch. He appears, and Methuselah tells him what has happened. Enoch answers and says:

> The Lord will do a new thing in the earth. There will come a great destruction on the earth and a deluge for one year. This son who is born unto thee will be left on the earth, and his three children will be saved with him, when all mankind that are on the earth shall die. And there will be a great punishment on the earth, and the earth will be cleansed from all impurity.

Enoch then decrees that the child should be named Noah, and promises Methuselah that Noah and his children will be safe from the coming disaster. Methuselah calls the child Noah, "for he would cause the earth to rejoice in compensation for all the destruction." Noah's future is determined. He is set apart for greatness.

Noah's miraculous birth story and Enoch's proclamation predict Noah's future importance. Hope still claims all might be well again with Noah's presence and help. "Noah grew up in righteousness and followed zealously in the ways of truth which Methuselah taught him; but the others of the people practiced wickedness towards God and deceit towards one another." Despite the men of God who serve as examples and who work for their salvation, the human condition is difficult to repair.

Jewish folktales record that the world changed the moment Noah was born. According to these tales, after Adam sinned God had cursed the world. Fields would not grow according to the seeds planted in them; when wheat was sown, oats would sprout and grow, for example. Adam and his descendants were not able to domesticate and control animals; Cows refused to give milk and oxen would not pull plows. Even the sea was uncooperative, raging at will across the earth. But with the birth of Noah, wrote Louis Ginzberg, "all returned to its state preceding the fall of man."

CREATION CONTINUES ITS FALL

Despite these positive changes, mankind's turn from God intensified after the birth of Noah. All the disobedience, the mingling of heavenly beings with the daughters of earth, the violence, and the idol worship served to push God to his limit. According to one Jewish legend, God sends Metatron (Enoch) to tell Shemhazai, one of the fallen angels, that He has decided to destroy the world with a flood. In another tale, related in the Talmud, God says,

According to legends, a great famine over the land since the time of Lamech ended with the birth of Noah.

"The whole earth is corrupt. I will destroy this man whom I have created, the fowls of the heaven and beasts of the earth, for the wickedness of man proves him undeserving of life, and I repent I have made him."

But God decides not to act until one righteous family remains. God does not want his creatures who remained faithful to see the horror of the punishment. "Noah found grace in the eyes of the Lord; and God selected Noah and his family from all the people on earth, to keep them alive

"The Lord saw how great man's wickedness on the earth had become, and that every inclination of the thoughts of his heart was only evil all the time. The Lord was grieved that he had made man on the earth, and his heart was filled with pain. So the Lord said, 'I will wipe mankind, whom I have created, from the face of the earth—men and animals, and creatures that move along the ground, and birds of the air—for I am grieved that I have made them'" (Genesis 6:5–7).

through the destruction which he designed," the Talmud, reports.

With ominous simplicity, the Talmud then lists the deaths of the righteous ones. Enosh, Kenan, and Mahalalel die, then Jared. Others, too, who had obeyed the Lord, die. The ticking of the clock that signals the end of it all grows louder and louder. But in the commentaries, the rabbis believe God has not quite given up.

In the 480th year of Noah's life, the word comes to Methuselah and Noah, saying: "Go forth, proclaim to all mankind, 'Thus saith the Lord: Turn from your evil inclinations, abandon your unrighteous ways, then may God forgive and spare you on the face of the earth. For thus saith the Eternal, one hundred and twenty years will I give ye to repent; if you forsake your evil ways, then will I forsake my intentions of destruction.'"

The God of Creation does not casually destroy what he has created. Hope is alive, if Noah and Methuselah are heard and obeyed. The creation, to God, is more than just a product. "The creation . . . is not an object built by a carpenter," writes Walter Brueggeman. "It is a vulnerable partner whose life is impacted by the voice of one who cares in tender but firm ways."

Perhaps Noah will be able to turn the disobedient, wayward world back to the Lord. But, thick and threatening, the storm clouds are gathering.

3

The Coming Disaster

Genesis bluntly states God's ultimate decision. God is grief-struck—even brokenhearted—seeing the great wickedness in thought and action. The Lord says, "I will blot out man whom I have created from the face of the ground, man and beast and creeping things and birds of the air, for I am sorry that I have made them" (Genesis 6:7).

A Too-Perfect World

The cosmic experiment has gone wrong, thanks to the people's abuse of their free will. It was not what God had intended. God desired righteous creatures. "Noah is living at a time when humanity is as yet undeveloped in its conception of righteousness," writes Karen Armstrong, a former nun who has written extensively on Judaism, Christianity, Islam, and other religions. "Indeed God is learning what He wants from the human race."

God wants this creation idea to work. But after seeing such dishonest, criminal, immoral lives, generation after generation, God can stand it no longer. For 120 years Noah and Methuselah try, even threatening the people with the consequences of total destruction. The Talmud reports: "Noah and Methuselah went forth and spoke these words of the Lord to the people. Every day, from morning until night, they addressed the people, but the people heeded not their words." The Qur'an describes how the people "thrust their fingers in their ears, and cover themselves with their garments, and persist and are big with pride" (Qur'an 71:7). In the Qur'an, Allah tells Noah to let the people do as they wish. Ignore them, Allah says. Their doom is already sealed.

THE END TIMES

God instructs Noah to marry and have children. Children are necessary to serve as the foundation for the new world coming. The rabbis surmise that Noah has held off having a family because he has not wanted to bring children into such a wicked world. Noah, always willing to obey, "did as God commanded him, and took to wife Naamah, the daughter of Enoch; and Noah was four hundred and ninety-eight years old."

Naamah soon conceived and bore three sons, Japheth, Ham, and Shem. The Talmud reports, "The lads grew up and walked in the way of God, as they were taught by Noah and Methuselah. And in these days died Lamech, father of Noah."

God then tells his faithful servants, Noah and Methuselah, to warn the people again—one last chance. But their words of warning go unheeded.

According to the Talmud, the people have continued to misbehave because Methuselah, the last righteous man other than Noah, is still alive; Noah had said that God would not act as long as Methuselah lived. But, in the final years of the 120-year period, Methuselah does die. Time is up. The day of reckoning approaches.

Preacher and Prophet

When Noah first appeared on the scene, according to Jewish legend, he was immediately involved with Methuselah and Lamech in their attempts to turn the people back to God. Though Genesis is silent about this, only saying Noah obeyed all of God's commands, the Qur'an gives Noah a preacher's voice:

> My Lord, I have called my people night and day: But my call has only made them flee the more. . . . I have called to them aloud, then spoken to them in public and spoken to them in private. So I have said: Ask forgiveness of your Lord; surely he is ever forgiving. (Qur'an 71:5, 6, 8–10)

The New Testament calls Noah "a herald of righteousness" (2 Peter 2:5). Noah the preacher tries to inform the people, to teach them the way they need to behave.

A preacher's voice is also a prophetic voice, interpreting the signs of the times. Says Jewish theologian Abraham Heschel:

> The prophet is a man who feels fiercely. God has thrust a burden upon his soul. . . . God is raging in the prophet's words. . . . The prophet's word is a scream in the night. While the world is at ease and asleep, the prophet feels the blast from heaven.

And what a blast from heaven Noah felt! The prophetic voice of Noah is heard in the Qur'an, pleading with people to turn back to Allah: "I am a plain warner to you, to serve none but Allah. Verily I fear for you the chastisement of a painful day" (Qur'an 11:25, 26). However, prophets are often ignored or considered insane until the things they have proclaimed come to pass. This is the reaction of the people to Noah's message: "We see not but a mortal like us . . . nor do we see in you any superiority over us. . . . He is only a madman" (Qur'an 11:27, 28, 23:25).

"Madness, however, may be the effect of genius," com-

The three sons of Noah: Shem, Ham, and Japheth. In traditional Jewish, Christian, and Muslim teachings, these three were believed to be the ancestors of all the modern ethnic groups. According to this belief, the Semitic people of the Middle East are said to be descended from Shem; the people of Africa from Ham; and the people of Europe and Asia from Japheth.

mented Heschel. "[T]o the prophets it is inconceivable to go on living and not be aware of the Creator of the world." Noah's urgent words of warning cause his hearers to think he is out of his mind. And in addition to his words, how could Noah not be seen as mentally troubled for carrying out God's next directive?

How to Build an Ark

The preacher/prophet is about to receive another vocation. The Genesis account outlines Noah's next task: "I have determined to make an end of all flesh; for the earth is filled with violence through them; behold, I will destroy them with the earth. Make your self an ark of gopher wood" (Genesis 6:13–14a). Noah obeys the Lord and sets to work. Genesis provides the basic guidelines followed by Noah:

> Make rooms in the ark, and cover it inside and out with pitch. This is how you are to make it: the length of the ark three hundred cubits, its breadth fifty cubits, and its height thirty cubits. Make a roof for the ark, and finish it to a cubit above; and set the door of the ark in its side; make it with lower, second, and third decks. (Genesis 6:14b–16)

But without some experience, how did Noah do it? Genesis does not explain where Noah acquired the carpentry skills he would need to construct a boat. "God showed him," is the simple conclusion, but the rabbinic tradition also suggests Noah had possession of a valuable item left over from a former time.

An Instruction Manual

According to Jewish legend, Noah possesses a book that had once been owned by his forefather Adam. This book supposedly contained all the wisdom of heaven and earth. The holy book disappeared after Adam's death, but its location in a cave was revealed to Enoch in a dream. Enoch had gained all his knowledge of earth and heaven from it, had memorized it, and then had hidden it again. The legend goes that when God decided to flood the earth, he sent the archangel Raphael to Noah, saying:

> I give thee herewith the holy book, that all the secrets and mysteries written therein may be made manifest unto thee, and that thou mayest know how to fulfill its injunction in holiness, purity, modesty, and humbleness. Thou wilt learn from it how to build an ark of the wood of the gopher tree, wherein thou, and thy sons, and thy wife shall find protection.

Noah studied the book. He was filled with the Holy Spirit and suddenly knew exactly how to build the ark and gather the animals. He carried the book with him on the

Defining a Cubit

A cubit is typically the distance between the elbow and the middle finger. A common cubit was six handbreadths. A royal cubit, sometimes called a sanctuary cubit, was seven handbreadths. A handbreadth was the distance across four fingers.

In 2 Kings 20:20, there is a description of a water tunnel being built in Jerusalem. The length of the tunnel is given as 1,200 cubits. The tunnel, built in the time of King Hezekiah, still exists today. Archaeologists were able to compute the length of a cubit based on their measurements of the tunnel. Their computation found a cubit to be equal to 17.49 inches.

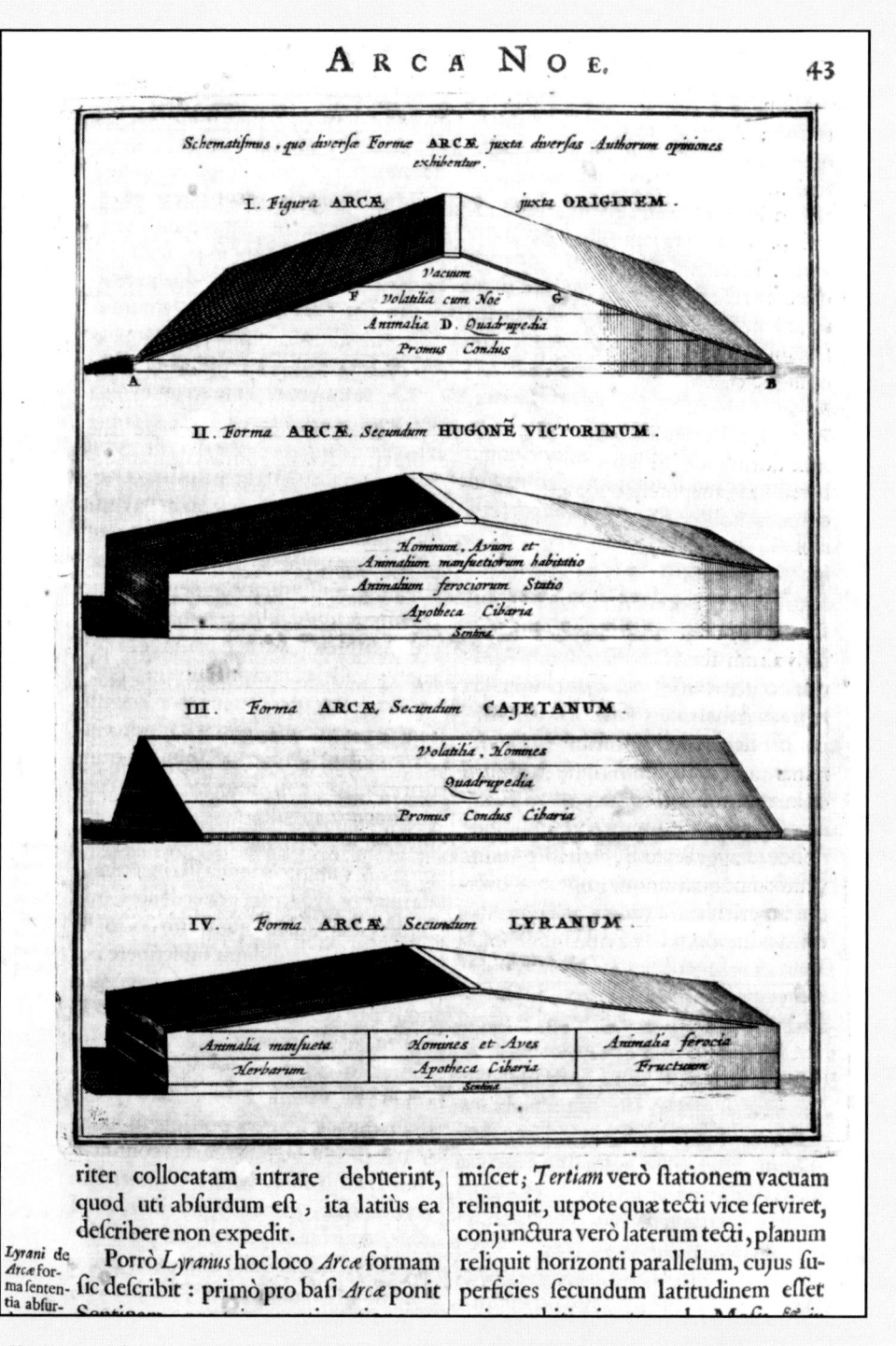

Illustration from a Dutch manual, circa 1675, describing the construction of the ark.

ark, where it changed into a timepiece to distinguish night from day. The legend says that after the Great Flood, Noah entrusted it to Shem, who gave it to Abraham. It then made its way from Jacob to Levi, Moses, Joshua, and finally Solomon, who learned his wisdom from it.

The book of Jubilees more simply states that Noah "made the ark in all respects as [God] commanded him (on the new moon of the first month)" (Jubilees 5:22).

The Qur'an notes that Noah built the ark according to the revelation of Allah, under Allah's watchful eyes (Qur'an 23:27). In any case, all of the sources agree that Noah was not alone or unaided. He had God's help, and all the knowledge of the ages.

By some accounts, the building of the ark occurred over many of the 120 years, giving the people plenty of time to repent of their sins. Some stories indicate that Noah began building the ark when he was 595 years old and that it was completed when he was 600 years old. Most traditions describe the ark as a large vessel, not a boat shape actually, but more of a rectangular prism. The Genesis description, converted to modern measurements, yields an ark 450 feet long (one and a half football fields), 75 feet broad, and 45 feet high, with a large door in the side. Windows surrounded the top edge, all covered by a roof to keep out the rain. Inside were rooms for the animals on three levels.

> The Qur'an describes the ark as made of planks and nails, built by Allah's revelation. Allah assures Noah that those individuals who are mocking him as he hammers will be, quite simply, drowned.

Noah Loses Heart

The apocryphal book of Enoch relates a story about Noah's anxiety during this time. Changes are occurring on earth hinting at the approaching disaster. The ark is nearly complete when Noah notices the earth is sinking. He goes to the ends of the earth and cries out the name of Enoch three times, begging to know the nature of the coming peril. There is "a great commotion" on earth, and a voice from heaven, Enoch's voice, saying, "Why hast thou cried unto me with a bitter cry and weeping?" (Enoch 65:5b). Enoch tells Noah the earth is ruined thanks to people learning the secrets of angels, the violence of Satan, all the secret powers of sorcery and witchcraft, and the knowledge of making molten images.

But Enoch comforts Noah and says:

> The Lord of Spirits knows that thou art pure, and guiltless of this reproach concerning the secrets. And He has destined thy name to be among the holy, and will preserve thee amongst those who dwell on the earth; And has destined thy righteous seed both for kingship and for great honours; And from thy seed shall proceed a fountain of the righteous and holy with number forever. (Enoch 65:11b–12)

Enoch proceeds to show Noah the angels of punishment, poised to let loose the waters beneath the earth to bring judgment and destruction. So Noah leaves Enoch and returns to his home. Noah knows he will be safe. (In this account, angels are credited with building the ark.)

The Coming of the Animals

The animals enter the ark in the Genesis account first as "two of every sort into the ark . . . male and female. Of the birds according to their kinds, and of the animals according to their kinds, of every creeping thing of the ground according to its kinds, two of every sort shall come in to you" (Genesis 6:19–20). God tells Noah to bring food as well. A few verses later, in the next chapter, we read a second description, to "take seven pairs of all clean animals, the male and his mate; and a pair of the animals that

The difference between God's instructions in Genesis 6:19 ("You are to bring into the ark two of all living creatures, male and female, to keep them alive with you") and Genesis 7:2-3 ("Take with you seven of every kind of clean animal, a male and its mate, and two of every kind of unclean animal, a male and its mate, and also seven of every kind of bird, male and female, to keep their various kinds alive throughout the earth") is often cited by textual critics as an illustration of the way in which the book of Genesis combines stories from multiple sources. Those who subscribe to the documentary hypothesis credit the first verse to the Priestly source, and the second passage to the Yahwist. However, it is also possible that the author of Genesis simply related the story in this way as a matter of style, and that it reflects God's clarification of his original instructions to Noah.

The animals enter the ark; painting by Edward Hicks, 1846.

are not clean, the male and his mate; and seven pairs of the birds of the air also, male and female, to keep their kind alive upon the face of all the earth" (Genesis 7:2–3). God gives Noah seven days to do this before the rain comes.

The Talmud records God as saying:

> Go thou with all thy household into the ark, and behold, I will gather to thee all the beasts and fowls, and they will surround the ark. Then place thyself in the doorway of the ark, and beasts and fowls will place themselves opposite to thee. Those that lie down before thee let thy sons lead into the ark, and those that remain standing thou shalt abandon.

Noah follows God's directive, as always, and the ark takes on passengers.

Rabbinic legend goes on to say Noah notices a lioness with her two cubs. All three crouch, until the cubs struggle with the mother. She stands up next to them. Noah leads the cubs on board the ark and leaves the mother outside. The rabbinic tales also mention the reem, an animal so large Noah cannot fit it into the ark. Noah ties it to the ark, and it runs (or perhaps swims) along behind.

Another Jewish legend says that two other peculiar creatures seek safety in the ark. First, falsehood comes asking to be saved. Noah denies this personification entrance, because he has no mate. Falsehood leaves and finds Misfortune. They approach the door and Noah lets them enter. Through this story, the rabbis explain that even after the Flood, evil will endure.

Storm Clouds Gather

For now, Noah's ark is complete. Noah has the assurance he and his family will be saved. The animals are aboard. Noah and his family enter. In the traditional Jewish folk tales, Noah hesitates outside; though he is more faithful than the people around him, his faith still falters. The water rises to his knees before he goes in. The Lord himself closes the great door.

The sound of thunder comes, and with it, the pounding of rain and the rushing of water. The foretold disaster is upon them.

4

The End of the World

People in modern times do not need to experience a flood to learn of its horror; the mass media transports viewers to the scenes of floods around the world. We have watched news reports about the terrible tsunami that battered communities throughout the Indian Ocean in December 2004, killing more than 225,000 people. In August 2005, Hurricane Katrina nearly erased New Orleans from the continent in a matter of hours, the force of its wind and water overwhelming everything. The agony of a flood—the total devastation, the obliteration of cities, the loss of life and possessions, the overwhelming power of water—is clear. Often, the only thing left for those who have experienced such a major disaster is to start over.

Ancient Floods

People in ancient Mesopotamia experienced flooding throughout their history. Evidence shows human activity in the Tigris and Euphrates river valleys eight thousand years ago. No longer nomads, these people had settled into the ebb and flow of a regular pattern of life. They learned the seasonal changes and requirements, inventing tools and implements to better their lives. They planted crops in the lush valley, fertile because of regular floods depositing rich silt over the land.

Memory lives in a people, and myth and legend often have their roots in an actual event, though the actual event may have been somewhat different than the epic material recalls. A massive flood, unforgettable in scope

Clay idols of Hindu gods stand amid the rubble of a village on the Indian island of Car Nicobar that was destroyed by a deadly tsunami, December 2004.

People of the 21st century need only view the impact of modern natural disasters to understand how life-altering a flood can be. This aerial view shows a flooded neighborhood in New Orleans, August 2005. Hurricane Katrina's high winds and heavy rains caused levees protecting the city to fail, allowing water from the Mississippi River and Lake Pontchartrain to flood about 80 percent of New Orleans. The storm also caused flooding and severe damage along the Gulf coast of the United States, from central Florida to Texas.

and effect, might have occurred in Mesopotamia at one time. In trying to understand what happened, the ancients would have told and retold tales about this disaster. These stories would preserve in an almost poetic form a natural occurrence. These tales grew and changed with the centuries, with details and names changing. Stories merged into one another. But the fact is, people remembered a great flood.

The Storm Begins

Genesis does not include details about the violence of raging floodwaters. The Biblical account simply says that, as the flood waters rose,

> Every living thing that moved on the earth perished—birds, livestock, wild animals, all the creatures that swarm over the earth, and all mankind. Everything on dry land that had the breath of life in its nostrils died. Every living thing on the face of the earth was wiped out; men and animals and the creatures that move along the ground and the birds of the air were wiped from the earth. Only Noah was left, and those with him in the ark (Genesis 7:21–23).

Jewish folklore provides additional details about about what happens when the rain begins to fall. Seven hundred thousand men come running, begging to be let on board, but Noah is resolute and refuses. He tells them they are going to be destroyed and asks why they did not repent when they had the opportunity. They claim to be ready now, but Noah says, "Too late." The crowd of sinners tries to force their way on the ark, but they are attacked by the wild beasts surrounding it. Some of these sinners are giants, and they tell Noah they know the water will never cover them. So God drops boiling hot rain down on them, scalding their skin. According to another tale, people try to plug up the streams of water using their own children; they are evil to the end.

Noah and the living creatures on the ark must endure rain for 40 days and 40 nights. And more than just rain; the Bible reports that "all the fountains of the great deep burst forth, and the windows of the heavens were opened" (Genesis 7:11b–12). Here the writer is drawing a parallel. The God of Creation, who moved over the face of the primal waters in the first chapter of Genesis, is at work in the Flood, using the primal waters above and below the earth to destroy it. The Flood marks a return to the chaos of pre-Creation.

As the ark is suspended on the water, time and creation seem suspended, allowing the cleansing to be complete. One commentator writes in a compelling way:

> We see water everywhere, as though the world had reverted to its primeval state at the dawn of Creation, when the waters of the deep submerged everything. Nothing remained of the teeming life that had burst forth upon the earth. Only a tiny point appears on the face of the terrible waters: the ark that preserves between its planks the seeds of life for the future.

Other sources also describe the origins of the Great Flood. The book of Jubilees reports: "And the Lord opened seven flood-gates of heaven, and the mouths of the fountains of the great deep, seven mouths in number; and the flood-gates began to pour down water from the heaven forty days and forty nights. And the fountains of the deep also sent up waters, until the whole world was full of water" (Jubilees 5:24, 25).

"The Deluge," an 1805 painting by the British artist Joseph Turner, attempts to capture the despair and hopelessness of humans as the Great Flood commences.

The Qur'an agrees, saying, "Then we opened the gates of heaven with water pouring down, and made water to flow forth in the land in springs, so the water gathered together according to a measure already ordained" (Qur'an 54:11, 12).

As the Flood raged and the ark rocked, the living inhabitants were shaken and frightened. A Jewish legend relates that at one point Noah cries out in prayer: "O Lord, help us, for we are not able to bear the evil that encompasses us. The billows surge . . . the streams of destruction make us afraid, and death stares us in the face . . . deliver us . . . redeem us and save us."

The legend also describes changes in the celestial spheres during the time of the Flood. The sun and moon give no light. The ark is illuminated by a precious stone that gives off light.

The waters submerge the highest mountains, blotting out every living thing. What a horrible scene outside the ark!

A Worldwide Flood?

Was Noah's Flood a worldwide flood? Most archaeologists and scientists do not believe that this is possible. Their examinations of the Earth's geology do not show evidence of a vast flood that wiped out almost all life on the planet. Experts have considered a wide variety of possible natural causes for a flood of worldwide proportion: earthquakes and tidal waves, melting glaciers, or tectonic activity that raised and lowered the land have all been ruled out as possible causes.

Despite the scientific evidence, many people still believe that Noah's flood literally covered the earth. Religious conservatives view the geologic and archaeological evidence with skepticism. They doubt scientific evidence that indicates the earth is billions of years old. They claim any appearance of age beyond the biblical maxi-

Caring for the Animals

Outside the ark, waves surged, and bodies floated. Inside, the animals demanded care. Rabbinic tradition credits Shem with explaining how hard it was to keep those animals alive. Noah and his sons had to feed animals they had never seen before, such as the zitka, so they needed to experiment to find what each creature would eat. The zitka did not eat the fruit offered it, but ate the worms that gathered inside. The lion had a fever. The urshana kindly told Noah he had seen how busy Noah was and did not want to trouble him about food. According to this folktale, to help deal with some of the problems associated with all the animals cooped up in the ark, Noah caused an elephant to give birth to a pig, which began to eat the filth piling up. He also rubbed the lion's nose and produced a cat that began to kill the rats infesting the ark, attracted by the filth.

mums is an act of God, meant to conceal the truth of the Creation from modern eyes. According to this view, the appearance of age in rocks may even be the result of the earth being totally immersed in water.

Textual critics have proposed that the issue may be a misunderstanding or incorrect interpretation. The Hebrew word for *earth* used in Genesis 6:17 is also translated "land" or "country" elsewhere in the Bible. As a result, many scholars and writers believe the Noah story—along with other Near Eastern Flood stories—can be traced back to an ancient event, probably a major flood that occurred in Mesopotamia.

Parallels with Other Flood Accounts

Flood stories abound in ancient cultures on every continent. Three appear at various times in the ancient Near East. Oldest is the Sumerian account of Ziusudra (sometimes spelled "Xiusudra"), with one copy found in archaeological excavations. It is believed to have been written around 1800 B.C.E. Another story from around this time is called the Atrahasis epic; this tale circulated in the ancient Mesopotamian city-state of Akkad, and was preserved in cuneiform tablets discovered at Nineveh. The best-known

---

Stories about the destruction of the earth by the gods exist in the sacred literature of other religions, including Zoroastrianism, a religion that emerged in Persia 2,500 to 3,000 years ago. According to Zoroastrian belief, the creator god Ahura Mazda decides to bring a great freeze upon the earth to control its runaway population. One man, Yima, is told to preserve the seeds of various species of trees and take shelter in an underground enclosure.

A fragment of the clay tablet containing the earliest known copy of the Gilgamesh epic. The compact cuneiform characters are extremely difficult to decipher. The 12 tablets containing the story of Gilgamesh were found in a royal library at Nineveh, the ancient capital of the Assyrian empire. (The ruins of this city are located in the northern part of modern-day Iraq.) Nineveh is mentioned numerous times in the Bible; Genesis 10:11 states that the city was built by a grandson of Noah.

of these stories is the Akkadian text of the Gilgamesh epic, found on clay tablets dated to the seventh century B.C.E.

Those who subscribe to the documentary hypothesis of Biblical composition believe that these Near Eastern flood stories predate the writing of the Genesis account and may have influenced it. There are striking similarities, but also many differences.

The Ziusudra story tells that the gods have decided to destroy mankind with a great flood. However, a Sumerian king named Ziusudra learns about the impending disaster. A section of the story (which was recorded on a clay tablet) is missing, but the tale does relate the flood rocking a huge boat that Ziusudra has built. The flood lasts for seven days, after which Ziusudra disembarks and offers a sacrifice to the gods.

The Atrahasis story tells of the rapid increase in population, which results in noise that troubles the gods. They first try to reduce the human population by infertility and famine; that does not work, so the gods settle on a flood instead. The hero of that tale, Atrahasis, is saved because he is favored by the god Ea. He builds a boat from reeds and takes his family and some animals aboard. The Atrahasis flood lasts seven days and seven nights, scaring the gods half to death with its intensity. When the flood ends, Atrahasis thanks the gods for preserving his life and offers sacrifices.

The Gilgamesh epic is probably derived in part from the Atrahasis story (which may itself have been rooted in the Ziusudra account). When the gods decide to flood the earth, the god Ea decides to save a man named Utnapishtim because he likes him, so he tells him how to build a boat. Utnapishtim needs to finish the boat in seven

Archaeologists have discovered other references to a Great Flood in their excavations of the Middle East. An account of the flood by Berossus, a Babylonian priest of the third century, has been lost, but parts of the tale have been quoted in other sources. Berossus's tale is similar to the Ziusudra account. The ancient Assyrian king Ashurbanipal wrote of studying stone inscriptions from before the Flood. The Sumerian King List, a document that lists ancient rulers, is interrupted by the line "then the Flood swept thereover." It seems to correspond to an actual flood in Sumeria that occurred around 2900 B.C.E.

days. He brings family, animals, and some craftspeople with him. Gilgamesh, a great king of Mesopotamia, later meets Utnapishtim, who has been granted immortality by the gods.

The similarities are obvious. The tales, including Noah's tale, may go back to a common source.

When Hope Overcomes Despair

This lonely picture, a tiny floating speck of life tossed on the waves amid a mass of death and destruction, has great theological impact. It teaches that humans have no control over their destinies; they are saved only through trust in God and obedience to His commands.

The words of hopelessness and despair spoken by the prophet Jeremiah at the time of the Babylonian exile, could easily have been spoken by Noah:

> I looked on the earth, and lo, it was waste and void; and to the heavens, and they had no light.
> I looked on the mountains, and lo, they were quaking, and all the hills moved to and fro.
> I looked, and lo, there was no man, and all the birds of the air had fled.
> I looked, and lo, the fruitful land was a desert, before the Lord, before his fierce anger. (Jeremiah 4:23–26)

The people of Israel who endured the Exile understood the isolation of the ark. The story of Noah would have had special meaning for them. Clinging to each other in a foreign land, trying to preserve their identity, was not different than what those passengers aboard the ark needed to do.

But change is in the air—a change moving the focus from the Flood and aiming at a new truth. It is a change in God himself, leading to the new creation.

5

A Saving Memory

The first few words of chapter 8 in Genesis are the turning point for the story of Noah and the crisis at hand: "And God remembered Noah" (Genesis 8:1a). Four words ending the destruction. Four words pointing to the new creation.

THE POWER TO CHANGE

Walter Brueggemann writes that the story of Noah is about "God's peculiar way of transforming [the world] . . . [that] God can [not only] change his mind and condemn what he's made; he can also rescue what he's condemned." God turns toward his people in a new way.

God remembers Noah and things begin to happen—for the better! "And God made a wind blow over the earth, and the waters subsided; the fountains of the deep and the windows of the heavens were closed, the rain from the heavens was restrained, and the waters receded from the earth continually. At the end of a hundred and fifty days the waters had abated" (Genesis 8:1b–3).

The Hebrew word for wind or spirit is *ruah*. It was *ruah* moving out over the waters in the Creation story in chapter 1 of Genesis. The word used by later Christian writers is translated as *pneuma*, or "spirit." The Spirit of God again moves out over the primal waters, just as in the first creation, to form a new creation.

When God remembers, it is a great and powerful act. The Orthodox Jewish scholar Blu Greenberg notes, "God remembers how much God loves humanity, is dependent on humans, and needs the relationship with them." The Flood is over. The waters recede.

Detail of a miniature Arab painting that depicts Noah's ark with animals peering from portholes on the side. The ark has distinctly Arab features, such as the lateen (triangular) sail. According to the Qur'an, Allah says, "Peace be to Noah among the nations! Thus indeed do We reward the doers of good. Surely he was of Our believing servants. Then We drowned the others" (Qur'an 37:79–82).

Sheep graze on the wide plains below Ararat, whose volcanic cone would be solitary but for Kucuk Agri Dagi ("Little Ararat") to the right. Many people believe this region is the place where Noah's ark came to rest as the flood waters receded.

LAND HO!

Genesis now describes the ark's landing. The mountaintops are visible shortly after the ark runs aground upon "the mountains of Ararat" (Genesis 8:4). Here, Ararat describes a region, rather than a peak. There is great dispute about just where that place might have been.

Modern-day adventurers who dub themselves "arkeologists" search for the remnants of Noah's ark. Many of these ark seekers center their search on a single peak, Agri Dagi in Armenia, the mountain they believe is the biblical Mount Ararat. But numerous other possible landing spots have been identified throughout the Middle East. Armenia, Turkey, Iran, Iraq, Saudi Arabia—all claim landing sites for the ark. Alleged artifacts have been discovered, but scientific dating indicates the artifacts are much younger than the ark of Noah could be. Despite the claim of Web sites, films, and many published books, no conclusive evidence of the ark's landing place or existence has been found to date. But believers have continued the search.

A modern scholar writes of the "arkeologists":

> [Their] books are flawed by misunderstandings and misuse of the ancient sources, by the use of "evidence" that most other investigators have discredited, and by a failure to investigate the accuracy of some of the tests used. . . . Some of the ark searchers seem to have made up their minds prior to an objective examination of the evidence.

While the search for the ark is interesting, to religious scholars it is a diversion. It is more important, they note, to remember the meaning of Noah's story than it is to find the physical remains of the ark.

HELPFUL BIRDS

In the scriptural account, once the ark runs aground and the mountains are visible, Noah sends various birds out to check the conditions. He sends a raven, which does not return. He then sends a dove three times, at seven-day intervals. First it returns because no landing site is available. Next it returns carrying an olive branch. Finally, it does not return.

The Jewish writer Isaac Singer tells a beautiful tale about why the dove was selected to be sent out by Noah. According to Singer's story, before the flood the animals heard that Noah would only select certain animals to come aboard the ark. The animals approached him, each bragging about its specific strengths in an overbearing way. Only the dove waited quietly in the background.

Detail from a 13th-century Byzantine-style mosaic in the Basilica of St. Mark, Venice, Italy, depicting Noah releasing a white dove. In New Testament literature, the dove retains special significance as a messenger and symbol of peace. At the baptism of Jesus, the Spirit of God descends like a dove, and a heavenly voice is heard.

Noah assures the animals all will be taken, then selects the dove for its special qualities as a bird of peace.

The Jewish legends provide more detail. According to these tales, Noah wants to send the raven out, but the raven argues with Noah. He does not want to leave the ark, claiming that both God and Noah hate him. Because the raven is an unclean animal (not supposed to be eaten), there are only two pairs of ravens on the ark. The raven tries to convince Noah that the world would be a far poorer place if he should perish in dangerous, unexplored territory. Finally the raven goes. However, he shirks his duty, so Noah sends the dove. According to this tale, the dove returns with an olive leaf taken from a tree growing on the Mount of Olives in Jerusalem.

Now assured the waters are dried up, Noah, according to Jewish legend, waits until he receives God's command before leaving. In his heart, Noah remains totally obedient. God told him when to enter the ark, and he trusts God to tell him when to leave. According to the Genesis account, God commands Noah and the entire entourage to leave the ark, so Noah obeys.

The World After the Flood

The aftermath of a flood, modern or biblical, is not a pretty sight. Stinking muck has replaced firm soil. Lifeless bodies litter the ground. Everything is changed. In the rabbinic commentary, Noah looks on this scene and weeps. He cries out in anger to God:

> "O Lord of the world! Thou art called the Merciful, and Thou shouldst have had mercy upon Thy creatures."
>
> God answered and said, "O thou foolish shepherd, now thou speakest to Me?"

God reminds Noah how He had complimented Noah's righteous behavior and had shared with him the plan to Flood the world. At that time, God says, Noah eagerly built the ark to save himself but did not worry about the fate of the world.

Some Jewish commentators do not hold Noah in high regard, because before the flood he did not argue with God to save the people. The eleventh-century Jewish rabbi Rashi taught that while Noah may have been considered righteous in his own generation (when all men were filled with sin), he would have been considered a "nobody" in Abraham's generation. Later in Genesis, Noah's descendant Abraham cares enough about other people to argue with God and question God's motives. Abraham tried to talk God out of destroying Sodom and Gomorrah, for instance. By contrast, Noah in Genesis is meek, mild, and obedient. He does what God says without question, never defending life on earth or pleading for mercy.

A Devotional Response

Noah's first act after leaving the ark is to take clean animals and build an altar and offer a sacrifice to God. Genesis 8:20–21 describes Noah's sacrifice in this way:

> Then Noah built an altar to the Lord and, taking some of all the clean animals and clean birds, he sacrificed burnt offerings on it. The Lord smelled the pleasing aroma and said in his heart: "Never again will I curse the ground because of man, even though every inclination of his heart is evil from childhood. And never again will I destroy all living creatures, as I have done."

Once again, Jewish folk tales flesh out the story. In fact, one legend even gives Noah's son Shem credit for actually making the sacrifice. According to this tale, Noah had been mauled by a lion while on the ark; because he was injured, he was unfit to serve in a priestly way.

Other legends provide additional details. One story explains that the sacrifice was required to pacify God after Noah accused Him of being merciless toward His Creation. Another story has Noah erecting his altar on the same place where Adam, Cain, and Abel had previously offered sacrifices to God. This, the legend continues, is the exact place where the altar would be located in the Temple sanctuary at Jerusalem—far from the mountains of Ararat, where the ark is said to have come to rest!

The ancient book of Jubilees offers more detail. "He made atonement for the earth and took a kid and made

68 Noah

Noah and his family offer a sacrifice to God. According to Jewish legends, the sacrifice consisted of an ox, a sheep, a goat, two doves, and two pigeons—all animals from among the seven pairs of clean animals that Noah had been instructed to take aboard the ark.

atonement by its blood for all the guilt of the earth; And he placed the fat . . . on the altar . . . and an ox, and a goat, and a sheep and kids, and salt, and a turtle dove, and the young of a dove, and placed a burnt sacrifice on the altar" (Jubilees 2–3). Then Noah poured oil, wine, and frankincense over it all and lit it. And the Lord smelled the good smell of it. Noah's first act in this new world was to offer an act of worship. A sacrifice of thanksgiving is a logical response to surviving death.

One modern rabbi, Burt Visotzky, suggests that Noah does not offer this sacrifice in love and praise, but in the hopes of appeasing God:

> Noah had just witnessed, in the most awesome of ways, how terrifying God can be. I think that as soon as he got off that boat, the first thing he did was to propitiate God in the best way possible. . . . That terror of God is something we don't often contend with. . . . Yes, we can approach God with love. But awe, trembling, fear—those are real ways of dealing with something wholly other, something terrifying.

A New Beginning

The world of Noah and his family has been washed away by the power of God. They stand in the presence of this God, awed and overwhelmed. But a new wind is blowing. As the fire crackles and consumes the sacrifice, the world is moving toward a new relationship. God himself is changed.

The Creator God has shown by his saving act that he is willing to continue with humanity. God remembers his promise to save Noah and the inhabitants of the ark. As biblical scholar Bernhard Anderson observes, the world stands on the brink of a "new age . . . a new creation in which the relations among human beings, nonhuman creatures, and their environment will be reordered."

The animals are dispersing. Noah and his family are warmed by the fragrant flames. The breath of God is in their faces, and they prepare to face a new world. Noah, the unlikely survivor, is about to become wealthy beyond comprehension. Noah and his family have become the inheritors of the world.

6

NEW CREATION AND FUTURE BLESSINGS

The smell of the roasting sacrifice has drawn God in, and it changes God's heart. God will never again destroy every living creature. He is moving in a new direction related to his created ones, even though humans have shown themselves to be full of flaws. The new creation is possible because God adjusts the relationship; he approaches humanity from another direction. Blu Greenberg states,

> In the beginning God was a perfectionist. In desperation, God would rather destroy His creation than accept it as less than perfect. But then, probably out of love and a sense of loss, God promises to accept human beings the way they are . . . and promises never to destroy them again. So the story of Noah is about God growing into the relationship, maturing in it . . . that's what a covenant is—a never-to-be broken relationship, no matter who falls off the side.

NEW WAYS IN THE NEW CREATION

God blesses Noah and his sons, issuing the charge Adam heard generations before: "Be fruitful and multiply, and fill the earth" (Genesis 9:1). Noah is given dominion over all living things. He and his family are the royal family, the rulers of the world. Noah becomes the new Adam, the new father of the human race.

Noah is wealthy with the gift of the earth and all that is in it. But in this new world, there are rules to follow. According to the Talmud, God gives Noah seven precepts of morality for all humanity to follow. These are known as the Noahide laws.

Two of the requirements of God's new covenant with man are listed in the Genesis account. These are laws against murder, and setting out the basic dietary requirements that would eventually be codified into the kosher laws of Judaism. In Genesis, God tells Noah:

> But you must not eat meat that has its lifeblood still in it. And for your lifeblood I will surely demand an accounting. I will demand an accounting from every animal. And from each man, too, I will demand an accounting for the life of his fellow man.
>
> Whoever sheds the blood of man,
>   by man shall his blood be shed;
>   for in the image of God
>   has God made man. (Genesis 9:4–6)

Other laws are outlined in the Talmud: worship only God, and not idols. Do not steal. Avoid sexual immorality, promiscuity, or adultery. Do not blaspheme God's name. Establish courts so that God's laws are enforced fairly, providing justice to all humanity.

After God created the heavens and earth, he gave simple instructions to Adam: Go, subdue the earth, and live it up—but do not touch that tree! Adam's inability to follow the rules led to creation's downfall. To Noah came laws meant to make God's new covenant work. This new king will rule differently than Adam, his predecessor.

There is a new spiritual relationship, a kingship within a framework. It is unlike the first creation. There is, according to Bernhard Anderson, "an open ended future in which God not only upholds the order of creation but continues to work creatively in the history that takes place on earth. God, who created in the beginning, creates the new thing."

The book of Jubilees says, "And [Noah] made a covenant before the Lord God for ever throughout all the generations of the earth" (Jubilees 6:10). Over succeeding generations, God would modify His covenant and add to the list of rules.

A Promise for the Future

This new covenant comes with a promise of permanence, visible in the heavens. "I establish my covenant with you, that never again shall all flesh be cut off by the waters of a flood, and never again shall there be a flood to destroy the earth. And God said, 'This is the sign of the covenant . . . for all future generations: I set my bow [rainbow] in the cloud, and it shall be a sign of the covenant between me and the earth'" (Genesis 9:9–14).

The word *bow* in this case means a bow that is the weapon of war. God hangs up his weapon; God is no longer in conflict with his creation and promises never again to destroy it. Ancients interpreted the rainbow as the hunting bow of God, hung up, as it were, on the wall—retired. The rabbinic legends promise that no matter how

The rainbow—God's promise that he will never again destroy His creation.

evil humankind becomes again, the rainbow reminds God and humanity their sins will not destroy them. In fact, report the rabbis, after the Flood, humans were sometimes so pious the bow was not even visible.

Other writings require regular remembrance of the covenant between God and Noah. The covenant must be celebrated, "for it was ordained and written on the heavenly tables, [to] renew the covenant every year. And this whole festival was celebrated in heaven from the day of creation till the days of Noah . . . and Noah and his sons observed it . . . to the day of Noah's death" (Jubilees 6:18). This is the root of the Jewish Festival of Weeks, later transferred to commemorate the giving of the law on Mount Sinai. After a time, Noah's sons gave up the celebration. But Abraham took up the celebration in future days, as did Isaac and Jacob.

Noah's wayward sons who so quickly forget to honor the festivals illustrate how some things in creation never change. The tendency to wander away from God, to break promises, remains. But in this new relationship there are some guarantees. The bow in the clouds serves to remind humanity of the promise, and it will remind God to honor his side of the bargain.

This feeling is echoed in the prophecy of Isaiah, preaching to the exiles to whom the primeval history was addressed:

> The Lord says, "For this is like the days of Noah to me: as I swore that the waters of Noah should no more go over the earth, so I have sworn that I will not be angry with you and will not rebuke you. For the mountains may depart and hills be removed, but my steadfast love shall not depart from you, and my covenant of peace shall not be removed" (Isaiah 54:9, 10).

The people of Israel returning from exile in Babylon could find peace in this story. As Noah and his family stood under the rainbow of God's peace, they, too, would experience a new beginning.

THE KING DIVIDES THE EARTH

Genesis concludes the story of the Flood by naming the sons of Noah, identifying them as the ones who, with their descendants, populated earth.

The division of the land proceeds, and what more fitting act should fall to Noah, new king of the world? His wealth—his dominion over all creation, his power to divide the land by his will—is detailed in the rabbinic legends and other sacred texts. Chapter 10 of Genesis concerns itself with the generations of the sons of Noah and their sons, kings who established their kingdoms over the whole earth and are symbolically linked to all the peoples of the world.

The Genesis account begins with the genealogy of Japheth, listing the succeeding generations, identifying Japheth as the originator of "the coastland people" (Genesis 10:2–5). Ham's offspring are listed next, a notable one being Nimrod, a mighty hunter. Nimrod goes on to become the founder of great cities like Nineveh. Canaan, the grandson of Noah, becomes the father of the Canaanite people. Shem is the father of the Semitic people. Among his offspring is a man named Eber, and it is from Eber that the Hebrew people are identified. Like his brothers, Shem and his offspring spread out over the land.

Jewish legends fill in the spaces left out in the scriptural account. They give the date of the distribution of the land as the year 1569 after the Creation. According to one folktale, Noah, closely observed by an angel, has his sons draw lots for the land. Shem pulls the slip "awarding him

Stained glass window depicting Noah's three sons dividing the earth.

the middle of earth, including the Holy of Holies in the Temple, Mount Sinai, the middle point of the desert, and Mount Zion." Ham gets the south lot, a desert land, and Japheth's sector, to the north, is cold. Ham is ancestor of dark-skinned people, and Japheth father to tribes that will align with Israel in the future.

The book of Jubilees describes how the sons of Noah further divide land, islands, nations, and languages among their own sons. Japheth gets 44 lands, 33 islands, 22 languages, and five kinds of writing. Ham receives 34 lands, 33 islands, 24 languages, and five kinds of writing. Shem's inheritance is 26 lands, 33 islands, 26 languages, and six kinds of writing. One of Shem's languages is Hebrew, language of the people of Israel and its holy book, the Torah.

According to the book of Jubilees, Noah warns his descendants that they should not think of taking territory that he has given to someone else. Noah says that any tribe that attempts this will be cursed.

NOAH'S CHALLENGE TO HIS SONS AND THE PRESENCE OF EVIL

The rabbis detail Noah's instructions to his children and their offspring. According to Jewish folktales, Noah warns them against evil living, such as the behavior that brought the Flood. He reminds them about the laws given after the Flood, especially the law against murder.

Noah does what all elders do at the end of their lives. He reminds the people of their history, of their need to honor the covenant; he links them to their ancestors: "For thus did Enoch . . . exhort his son Methuselah, and Methuselah his son Lamech, and Lamech delivered all unto me . . . and now I do exhort you, my children."

Noah reminds them of their duty to honor God on a regular basis; outlining the festivals will help them to remember the great and powerful acts of the Lord. Included was a law not to eat the fruit of a tree for the first three years it bears. The fourth year of the tree's productivity, the fruit would belong to the priests, who would offer a portion of it as a sacrifice. In the fifth year, the fruit could be eaten by all members of the community.

Noah's fears about things falling apart are well founded. According to the book of Jubilees, evil spirits soon begin to tempt Noah's sons and their children:

> The unclean demons began to lead astray the children of the sons of Noah; and to make to err and destroy them. And the sons of Noah came to Noah their father, and they told him concerning the demons which were, leading astray and blinding

The so-called Nergal Gate at Nineveh, which was excavated in the mid-19th century and reconstructed during the 20th century. Archaeological evidence indicates that the city of Nineveh was built about 4,000 years ago. This important Mesopotamian city, said to have been built by a descendant of Noah's son Ham, is mentioned numerous times in the Bible.

and slaying his sons' sons. And he prayed before the Lord his God, and said:

God of the spirits of all flesh, who hast shown mercy unto me, And hast saved me and my sons from the waters of the flood, and hast not caused me to perish as Thou didst the sons of perdition;

For Thy grace hath been great towards me, and great hath been Thy mercy to my soul; let Thy grace be lift up upon my sons, and let not wicked spirits rule over them lest they should destroy them from the earth.

But do Thou bless me and my sons, that we may increase and multiply and replenish the earth. (Jubilees 10:1–3)

Noah asks God to drive away all the evil spirits. However, according to the tale in Jubilees, the head demon, Mastema, makes a deal with the Lord, who leaves one-tenth of the demons behind to do Satan's bidding on earth.

In a related folktale, one of these demons is ordered to teach Noah how to cure all the diseases brought on by demons. Noah preserves this knowledge in a book, which is eventually given to his son Shem. In this way, the knowledge of medicine is passed to learned men. All goes well until one of the medical sages decides to search for some wood from the tree of life from the Garden of Eden. The Jewish scholar Louis Ginzberg writes, "When they arrived at the spot, they found healing trees and wood of the tree of life, but when they were in the act of stretching forth their hands to gather what they desired, lightning darted out . . . smote them to the ground, and they were all burnt. With them disappeared all knowledge of medicine." Legendary material frequently reminds the faithful of the result of seeking knowledge meant for God and not humankind.

The rabbinical commentary notes that before Noah dies, the descendants of Shem, Ham, and Japheth appoint princes over each of their territories, establishing links to Nimrod (from Ham; founder of Ninevah and Babylon), Joktan (from Shem), and Phenech (from Japheth). These individuals point toward the end of the primeval history. The world's population has exploded. According to the legends, 10 years before the death of Noah, tens of millions of people are alive.

NOAH OF THE VINEYARD

With the Flood over and promises of the new creation in place, another chapter opens in Noah's life. God's creatures are on a different path and in a renewed relationship with God. The path will continue until the call of Abraham, a few generations from now. This in-between time begins with an unusual story of Noah, a tiller of the soil (farmer), and his vineyard.

NOAH PLANTS A VINEYARD

Like Adam generations earlier, Noah receives the command to subdue the earth. His responsibility is to manage earth's agricultural possibilities; it is Noah's job to see that the earth fulfills its potential to grow abundantly. He is the new Adam.

As Genesis presents it, Noah is "the first tiller of the soil" and the one who "planted a vineyard" (Genesis 9:20). Noah works the land, plants a vineyard, and makes wine.

Noah of the Vineyard

The book of Jubilees offers more detail. According to that source, Noah is said to have planted the vines on the mountain where the ark landed. They bore fruit after four years. Noah made wine, letting it age for a year. "And he celebrated with joy the day of this feast, and he made a burnt sacrifice unto the Lord . . . and caused a sweet savour to ascend acceptable before the Lord his God. And he rejoiced and drank of this wine, he and his children with joy" (Jubilees 7:6). The account in Genesis, however, does not mention this religious sacrifice or describe how Noah's children also enjoy the festivities.

SOMETHING HAPPENED IN THE TENT

When evening comes, Noah collapses in his tent in a wine-induced stupor. His youngest son, Ham, who is the father of a child named Canaan, comes in the tent and discovers Noah, naked. He runs to get his brothers, who enter the tent backward so they do not have to see their father in this embarrassing situation. But not Ham. He strides in facing front. Shem and Japheth cover Noah with a garment. This is definitely not one of Noah's proudest moments.

Noah wakes up and realizes what has happened. He says, "Cursed be Canaan! The lowest of slaves shall he be to his brothers." And also, "Blessed be the Lord, the

According to a legend reported in the Talmud, the grapevine Noah planted had been taken by Adam from paradise after the fall.

God of Shem; May Canaan be the slave of Shem. May God extend the territory of Japheth; May Japheth live in the tents of Shem; and may Canaan be his slave" (Genesis 9:25–27).

It is hard to see what prompted such an angry outburst from Noah. Perhaps it is because Ham's behavior violates God's law to "honor thy father and thy mother," which centuries later would be given to the Israelites as a commandment in Exodus 20:12. Perhaps Ham mocked his father to his brothers, and when Noah learned of this disrespect, he responded with a curse.

Winemaking in Biblical Times

In Psalms 104:15 we read that wine is a drink to "gladden the hearts of men." Wine was highly prized in Old Testament times. It was present at weddings, festivals, and banquets. In fact, the word for banquet, *mishteh*, can also be translated "drinking." Wine was also served at every meal. To own a vineyard was a sign of peace and prosperity. The prestige of cultivating a vineyard rivaled that of growing olives and figs.

Canaanites were probably already making wine when the Hebrew people arrived in their land. The process was rather simple. A pair of basins was used, one above the other. These basins were either built with piles of rock, or carved out of the rock. Holes allowed the grape juice to flow from the top chamber to the bottom. The grapes were squeezed by treading, that is, mashing them with the feet. One or more men would be involved in treading, depending on the size of the chamber. Once the juice ran into the lower vat, it would be left to ferment, or it would be put into wineskins or large earthen jars to ferment. The sweet, freshly squeezed juice was called "must." Must alone was drunk; once fermentation was complete, the wine, with its alcoholic properties, would be enjoyed. Too much fermentation and a new product resulted: vinegar!

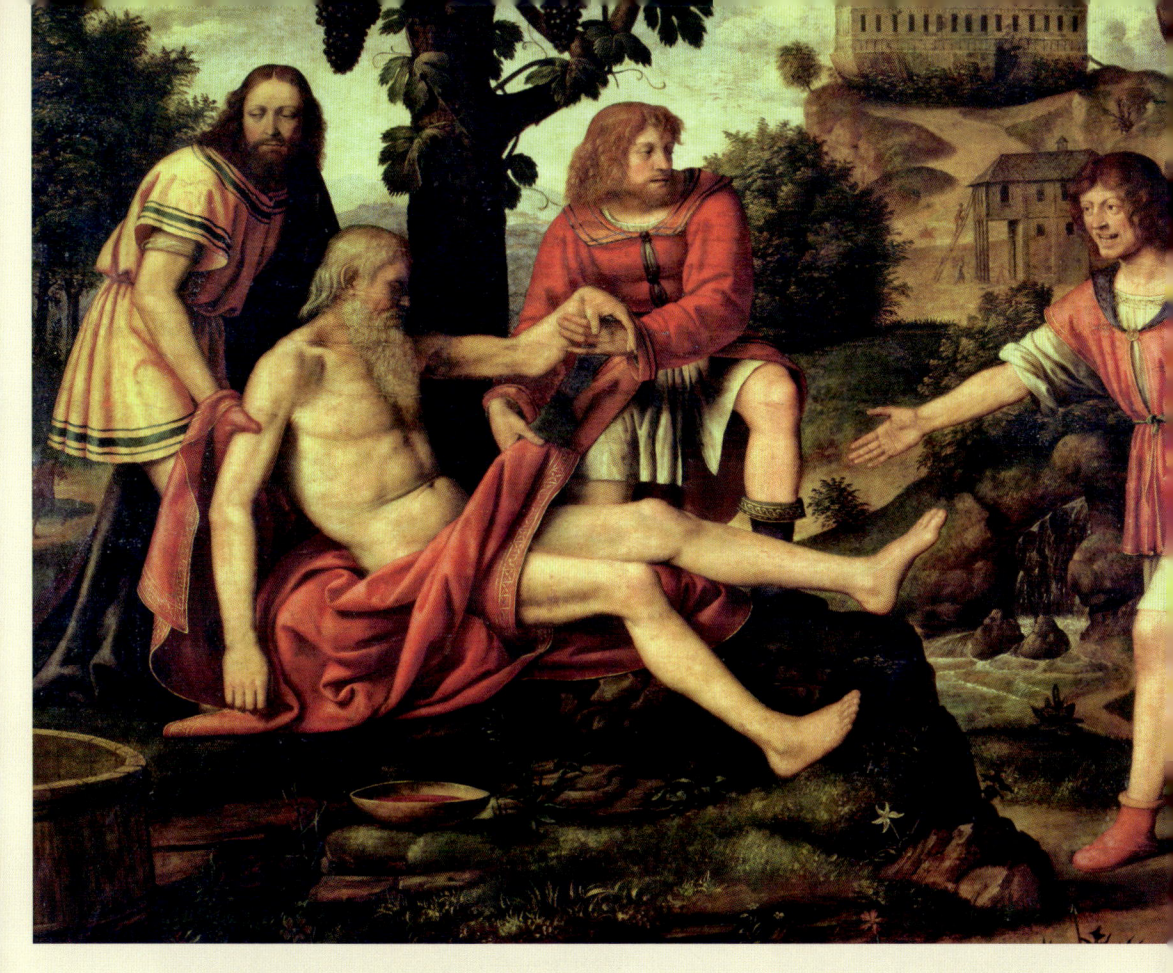

This Renaissance-era painting depicts Ham mocking his naked father, while Shem and Japheth attempt to cover Noah's nakedness.

Deeper Meanings

The description of Noah uncovered may have sexual overtones. In Leviticus 18:7–8, there are laws about proper sexual conduct; the Hebrew word for *uncovered* is used throughout, just as it is in this passage from Genesis. Accounts of the event in the Talmud and Jewish folklore support this view. They suggest Noah and his wife were engaged in marital relations when Ham walks in on them. Ham then goes to find his brothers, and disrespectfully reminds Shem and Japheth how the first man, Adam, had two sons, and one killed the other. Now their father, Noah, is inside that tent trying to enlarge the family once again! Noah is embarrassed that his privacy has been invaded and is indignant. According to the rabbis, Ham was still under protection of the post-Flood blessing, and thus immune to the curse, so Canaan, Noah's grandson, is punished for his father's offense.

Alternately, the vineyard story may have a deeper symbolic meaning—to explain and justify Israel's later conquest of Canaan. The story explains the favored position God has given to Israel (Semites—the descendants of Shem). It explains why the Semites and descendants of Japheth (who are probably allied with the Semites) flourish as civilizations, while the once powerful Canaanites blend in with their conquerors and disappear as a people.

For centuries, Noah's curse in Genesis 9:25-26 was used to justify racial prejudice. Ham is traditionally identified as the ancestor of black-skinned people (Africans), so the statement that Ham's descendents were cursed to be slaves was used to explain and support the African slave trade from the 15th to the 19th centuries. This is a misreading of the text: the curse is confined to a single branch of the Hamitic family. Today, most Biblical scholars agree that the curse was fulfilled in the Israelite conquest of Canaan. (It is worth noting that in Europe and North America during the 18th and 19th centuries, Christians were at the forefront of the movement to abolish slavery.)

Noah's curse carries into the future, notes Karen Armstrong. "[Noah] curses Canaan, leading the way for the new massacres of Joshua, where the people of Israel will be told to go into the land of Canaan and kill every single human being in the land."

THE DEATH OF NOAH

From this point, according to the Jewish legends, Noah's sons move out on their own. Ham, when he finds out his father had cursed him,

> fled ashamed, and with his family he settled in the city built by him . . . named for his wife. Jealous of his brother, Japheth followed his example. He likewise built a city which he named for his wife. . . . Shem was the only one of the sons of Noah who did not abandon him.

Genesis 9:28–29 reports that Noah lived for 350 years after the Flood, dying at the age of 950. The book of Jubilees provides the following details:

> Noah slept with his fathers, and was buried on Mount Lûbâr in the land of Ararat. Nine hundred and fifty years he completed in his life. . . . And in his life on earth he excelled the children of men save Enoch because of the righteousness, wherein he was perfect. (Jubilees 10:15)

Noah's story only occupies five chapters in Genesis, but Noah's impact is lasting and important. God never lets go of Noah or His created world. The message of this story is that God will never let His people go, either. Noah fulfills the promise of a new creation—a promise beyond disaster. Noah was saved, and so are we.

Statue of Noah holding the ark, from the cathedral in Cologne, Germany.

Understanding Noah Today

Noah is one of the most familiar and beloved of all biblical figures. Noah stands out because of his sheer goodness; he saves his family and all the animals when God decides to wipe out creation and start over. Noah is a comforting figure, as the Hebrew root of his name implies. The picture of Noah, floating in the animal-warmed ark, lanterns swaying, cattle lowing, provides an image of peace and contentment.

The Genesis account describes the ark as having three decks, with rooms for the animals. A 17th-century Jesuit, Athanasius Kircher, drew up a floor plan for the ark based on the biblical dimensions. According to Kircher's blueprint, each deck contained animals, provisions for the trip, and tools and implements for the future. Noah's family even had their own bedrooms, a kitchen, and a dining room. A bit imaginative, perhaps, but this example illustrates the need of people across the ages to fully understand this strange story and imagine how Noah's voyage could have happened. The scriptural account is slim, so over millennia scholars and sages have tried to fill in gaps in the story.

THE SEARCH FOR NOAH

At one time, in western civilization the Bible was considered the framework for all history. Sir Walter Raleigh (1552–1618) once defended the historical nature of Noah's flood based on his idea that only 100 species of animals existed on earth at the time of the Flood; plenty of room could be found on the ark's three decks, plus space left over for food and Noah's family.

However, over the past several centuries, this notion has been challenged by new discoveries and interpretations of ancient material. Archaeologists and scholars have applied modern scientific methods in an effort to learn more about the origins and validity of Biblical stories. "But scientists increasingly came to see the naiveté of the picture, not only in regard to animals but man himself," writes Bernhard Anderson.

Since the mid-1800s, many individuals and groups have attempted to find the remains of Noah's ark—definitive proof the story's truth. Much of this activity has centered on Mount Ararat in Turkey or its nearby peak, Agri Dagi in Armenia.

Some of the searchers have unearthed chunks of wood that suggest the ark. For example, in 1955 and 1969 French explorer Fernand Navarra produced wood beams that he claimed to have found on Mount Ararat, causing great interest. However, the pieces were carbon-dated and found to be about 1,400 years old—not old enough to match the biblical time frame of the Great Flood. In addition, a guide on the expedition later claimed that Navarra

Mount Ararat, the peak where some people believe Noah's ark came to rest after the Flood, looms behind this Christian monastery in Armenia.

had taken the pieces of wood to the mountain and faked their discovery. Indeed, over the centuries there have been numerous hoaxes connected with the discovery of pieces of Noah's ark.

In 1985, explorers Ron Wyatt and David Fasold found what they believed was the fossilized remains of Noah's ark at a spot in eastern Turkey about 18 miles away from Mount Ararat. They found several large stones with holes bored in them, which the men believed were drogue stones. In the ancient world, these heavy, flat stones would have been used as sea anchors; during a storm the drogues would be hung with ropes over the side of the ship, creating drag that would turn the vessel's bow into the waves. However, after further investigation Fasold decided that the ark was a natural geologic formation and that the stones had been ancient pagan monuments, rather than sea anchors.

One scholar, Lloyd Bailey, suggests that those who find artifacts on Mount Ararat or Agri Dagi may actually have stumbled across wood left there for other purposes. He cites several possibilities: the carrying up of crosses for erection on the mountain over many years; wooden containers left on the mountain; a large structure, the Monastery of Saint James; a chapel that was built further up the mountain from the monastery; and various huts or houses.

The strong desire to find something out there drives these groups to continue. They look for the proof that will solidify their view of creation, their belief that the Bible is true word for word. However, to date no solid evidence has been confirmed.

NEW EVIDENCE AND NEW ANALYSIS

By the late 1800s, biblical scholarship was taking a new direction. A German scholar named Julius Wellhausen had proposed his "documentary hypothesis," a theory that said the Bible was composed by several different authors over a period of hundreds of years.

In the dual accounts of the animals boarding the ark in Genesis (6:11–22 and 7:1–5), Wellhausen and other scholars recognized two styles of writing. They also noted the details of the Flood differed from one section to another. The story seemed to be retold. Scholars felt that these accounts represented two different hands involved in the writing. One source they named "J" for its tendency to name God "Jahveh" (the German spelling of Yahweh). This part of the text is believed to have been written around the time of David and Solomon (950 B.C.E.). The second story is attributed to a later writer or editor known as the Priestly source, or P. It dates to around 500–400 B.C.E., during the time of the return of Israel from Babylonian exile.

At around the same time, archaeological discoveries were being compared to Biblical accounts. For example, stone tablets containing the Babylonian flood myth were first deciphered in 1872. The awareness of a flood story that was different from the Bible's, but had come from the same region, had to be factored into belief systems.

While at first, this discovery seemed to conform the Bible's account of a Great Flood, people soon came to question the validity of this long-held belief. Biblical theologian F. H. Woods, writing in a theological dictionary of the Bible in early 1900, stated:

> Until comparatively recent times the belief in a deluge covering the whole world and destroying all men and animals except those . . . preserved in the ark was practically universal among Christians. The fossil remains of marine animals, and the Flood traditions common to people in so many

different parts of the worlds were appealed to as establishing the truth of the Bible story. Our increased knowledge of geology on the one hand and of comparative mythology on the other have now shown the little value of such evidence, and on these and other grounds this belief has now been surrendered by most biblical scholars as untenable.

In the late 1920s and early 1930s, Sir Leonard Wooley and others discovered flood deposits in the region of the Tigris and Euphrates rivers. The flood deposits varied in thickness up to 11 or 12 feet of freshwater silt. Though first thought to be evidence of Noah's Flood, they were in

Modern Biblical Criticism

There are three main types of biblical criticism used in scholarly circles today. Each has its roots in the work of particular scholars around the world.

Source criticism, sometimes called literary criticism, analyzes a scriptural text, identifying its meaningful parts and trying to determine their origins.

Form criticism recovers the roots of the text in the oral tradition and in its original setting in life.

Historical criticism traces the development of a text from its oral form to the current written form.

Redaction involves the investigation of how and why the redactor, or editor, of the ancient stories assembled them in the form that comes down to us today.

Scholarly work in biblical criticism involves much training and experience. Scholars study for decades to master the biblical languages, delving into the deep meanings of the texts. Understanding the Bible today with these methods is an evolving process in which scholars seek to determine the relevance of the Bible in modern times.

time shown to be proof only of local floods. Without concrete evidence of a worldwide flood or of a man named Noah, scholars looked for a way to interpret the stories rather than just take them at face value.

Interpreters associated with the Society of Biblical Literature used analytic methods to derive meaning from the texts. They used source criticism, form criticism, and historical criticism as methods that guided them through 20th-century scriptural studies.

This allowed for the identification of the Yahwist (J) and Priestly (P) sources contributing to the Flood stories. The J source contributes a folktale-like quality to the narrative, while the P source is concerned with intricate details, especially time. Words vary. The J source refers to a downpour (*gesem*) lasting 40 days and nights; the P source writes of a cosmic deluge (*mabbul*) in which the primal waters gush out from the ground and from behind the dome of the sky in an overwhelming wave. The sources come from different traditions, yet were merged by an editor's hand.

The J source stems from the time of the kingdoms of David and Solomon (982 B.C.E), a time of unification within the tribes of Israel. The stories had probably existed in oral form for centuries, but it was during this time that they were written in a permanent form. The Yahwist's account is Israel's national epic. The P source is dated to the time period after the fall of Israel in 587 B.C.E., reflecting the style and interests of the priestly circle.

CREATIVE DEBATE

Theologians since Augustine in the fifth century have puzzled over Genesis accounts. Modern-day theologians have gone to great lengths to explain the meaning of the language, offering theories of interpretation to avoid taking so much of Genesis, particularly the Creation accounts, so literally. Jeffery L. Sheler and Joannie M. Schrof, writing in an article entitled "The Creation," contend that to many otherwise devout Christians and Jews, "the Genesis account is understood as speaking metaphorically of the relationship between God and creation, rather than as a scientific or historical account."

Some scholars have attempted to use scientific analysis to support a literal reading of Genesis. "By tracing biblical genealogies, some adherents estimate that the earth came into being just 10,000 years ago," write Sheler and Schrof. "Fossils and geologic evidence of a much older earth, they

This piece of rock contains a fossilized trilobite, a sea creature that mainstream scientists believe became extinct about 250 million years ago. Some creationists, on the other hand, argue that fossils found in sedimentary rocks actually support their theory that the earth is less than 10,000 years old. According to this belief, fossils were created during Noah's flood when vast amounts of silt were suddenly dumped from churning waters, preserving the physical forms of creatures trapped underneath.

explain, are the result of Noah's flood, or . . . are simply part of an 'appearance of age' that God built into the universe." But this notion just does not work for many biblical theologians.

WHERE DOES NOAH FIT?

Change is evident in the field of biblical study, where scholars propose a new view about the nature of the source documents that make up Genesis. J and P sources were long believed to have been assembled by a redactor, a special kind of editor, who aligned the traditions together into one form. But a new idea, since the 1990s, is that the redactor, or R, was in fact a tradent, a theological writer utilizing ancient stories to put forward his own theological ideas—something new and dramatic. Biblical interpreters view the story of the Flood in the larger context of Genesis 1–11; they concern themselves with the message of new creation and new beginnings addressed to the people of Israel coming home after being in exile. They claim the message comes to modern hearers as well. Noah teaches less about an angry, destroying God and more about a God who saves. Noah, as the name says, brings a word of comfort.

Modern commentators on the Flood story emphasize again and again that God changes the way he deals with creation in the Noah story. Karen Armstrong goes as far as to say that "God is growing up in Genesis . . . [he is] a developing God." Carol Gilligan writes:

> God learns. What God learns is that terror and destruction don't change things and that the very evil in the story of Noah that God wanted to eradicate comes back. So God then makes a covenant to stay in relationship with us, and that creates the possibility of change.

96 *Noah*

American illustration of scenes from Noah's life, circa 1882. The story of Noah continues to fascinate children and adults alike.

The story of Noah represents the beginning of a new permanent relationship between God and humans. Permanence implies the need to change from time to time, adjusting the relationship so it endures.

In Conclusion

Neither scriptural nor nonscriptural accounts mention Noah's financial standing. No evidence exists that Noah was a millionaire. Noah lived long before money as we know it. Noah's spiritual connection with God in the days before the Flood was the only wealth he possessed.

Noah obeyed God. He preached righteousness. He tried to change the world and turn it back to God. He followed orders without argument or question. Modern opinion says he might have done more; when he learned God's destructive plan, perhaps he could have changed God's mind. But that was not his particular destiny. Noah and his family rode out the storm, and when the skies cleared, he built an altar. He led his family into a new time, a new creation, a new relationship with the Creator.

Noah was given the land, and divided it among his sons. He reminded the sons to be faithful and not forget what they had survived. Noah set in motion the generations stretching toward Abraham, and an everlasting covenant—a covenant that would be tested repeatedly, but would endure.

This is the wealth of Noah—the example his life teaches, whether the story is an actual account or a parable. Noah's life is an example of a person who lives as God intended. Noah remains a sign of hope for believers in the new creation.

Notes

CHAPTER 1: THE NOAH CONTROVERSY

p. 16: "The first eleven chapters of..." Walter Brueggemann, *Genesis* (Atlanta, GA: John Knox, 1982), p. 11.

p. 17: "In a district called Carra..." Lloyd R. Bailey, *Noah: The Person and the Story in History and Tradition*. (Columbia: University of South Carolina Press, 1989), p. 64.

p. 17: "The remains of the ark..." Bailey, *Noah*, 61.

p. 21: "the [primeval histories] are symbolic..." John H. Marks, *Interpreter's One-Volume Commentary on the Bible* (Nashville, TN: Abington, 1971), p. 11.

CHAPTER 2: CREATION IN CRISIS

p. 24: "The creator has a purpose..." Brueggemann, *Genesis*, 13.

p. 28: "bringing the world to its..." Louis Ginzberg, *The Legends of the Jews*, vol. 1 (Baltimore and London: Johns Hopkins University Press, 1998), p. 151.

p. 29: "Creation is undermined by..." David Patterson, *The Greatest Jewish Stories Ever Told* (Middle Village, NY: Jonathan David, 1997), p. 205.

p. 29: "Because all of humanity is..." Patterson, *The Greatest Jewish Stories Ever Told*, 205–6.

p. 29: "when creation does not listen..." Brueggemann, *Genesis*, 18.

p. 32: "grew regardless of..." H. Polano, ed. and trans., *The Talmud: Selections from the Contents of That Ancient Book, Its Commentaries, Teachings, Poetry and Legends* (1876). www.sacred-texts.com/jud/pol/index.htm.

Notes

p. 32: "The sinfulness of men was..." Ginzberg, *The Legends of the Jews*, p. 137.

p. 32: "[Methuselah] walked in the footsteps..." Ginzberg, *The Legends of the Jews*, p. 140.

p. 33: "was white as snow and..." Ginzberg, *The Legends of the Jews*, p. 145.

p. 33: "The Lord will do a..." Ginzberg, *The Legends of the Jews*, p. 146.

p. 34: "for he would cause the..." Ginzberg, *The Legends of the Jews*, p. 146.

p. 34: "Noah grew up in righteousness..." Polano, *The Talmud*, p. 22.

p. 34: "all returned to its state..." Ginzberg, *The Legends of the Jews*, p. 134.

p. 35: "The whole earth..." Polano, *The Talmud*, p. 22.

p. 35: "Noah found grace..." Polano, *The Talmud*, p. 22.

p. 37: "Go forth, proclaim..." Polano, *The Talmud*, p. 23.

p. 37: "The creation..." Brueggemann, *Genesis*, p. 18.

CHAPTER 3: THE COMING DISASTER

p. 38: "Noah is living at a..." Karen Armstrong, quoted in Moyers, *Genesis: A Living Conversation*, p. 134.

p. 40: "The prophet is a man..." Abraham Heschel, *The Prophets*, vol. 1 (New York: Harper Colophon, 1962), pp. 5, 16.

p. 41: "Madness, however, may be the..." Heschel, *The Prophets*, pp. 175, 185.

p. 43: "I give thee herewith..." Ginzberg, *The Legends of the Jews*, p. 156.

CHAPTER 4: THE END OF THE WORLD

p. 54: "We see water everywhere, as..." Umberto Cassuto, quoted in Bernhard Anderson, *From Creation to New Creation* (Eugene, OR: Wipf and Stock, 1994), pp. 141–42.

p. 55: "O Lord, help us, for..." Ginzberg, *The Legends of the Jews*, 162.

p. 59: "then the Flood swept thereover..." Bailey, *Noah*, p. 13.

Chapter 5: A Saving Memory

p. 61: "God's peculiar way of transforming..." Brueggemann, *Genesis*, pp. 75, 78, 85.

p. 62: "God remembers how much God..." Blu Greenberg, quoted in Moyers, *Genesis: A Living Conversation*, p. 140.

p. 64: "[Their] books are flawed by..." Bailey, *Noah*, p. 54.

p. 66: "O Lord of the world..." Ginzberg, *The Legends of the Jews*, p. 165.

p. 69: "Noah had just witnessed, in..." Burt Visotzky, quoted in Moyers, *Genesis: A Living Conversation*, pp. 143–44.

p. 69: "new age a new creation..." Anderson, *From Creation to New Creation*, p. 160.

Chapter 6: New Creation and Future Blessings

p. 70: "In the beginning God was..." Greenberg, quoted in Moyers, *Genesis: A Living Conversation*, p. 115.

p. 71: "an open ended future in..." Anderson, *From Creation to New Creation*, p. 164.

p. 75: "awarding him the middle of..." Ginzberg, *The Legends of the Jews*, p. 172.

p. 77: "For thus did Enoch..." Ginzberg, *The Legends of the Jews*, p. 171.

p. 79: "When they arrived . . ." Ginzberg, *The Legends of the Jews*, p. 177.

Chapter 7: Noah of the Vineyard

p. 84: "[Noah] curses Canaan, leading the..." Armstrong, quoted in Moyers, *Genesis: A Living Conversation*, p. 138.

p. 85: "fled ashamed, and with his..." Ginzberg, *The Legends of the Jews*, pp. 170, 171.

Chapter 8: Understanding Noah Today

p. 88: "But scientists increasingly came to..." Bernhard Anderson, *The Beginning of History: Genesis* (Nashville, TN: Abingdon, 1963), p. 93.

p. 91: "Until comparatively recent times the..." F. H. Woods, *A*

Dictionary of the Bible, vol. 2 (New York: Charles Scribner's Sons, 1906), p. 16.

p. 94: "the Genesis account is…" Jeffery L. Sheler and Joannie M. Schrof, "The Creation" *U.S. News & World Report* (December 23, 1991), p. 61.

p. 94: "By tracing biblical genealogies, some…" Sheler and Schrof, "The Creation," p. 59.

p. 95: "God is growing up in…" Armstrong, quoted in Moyers, *Genesis: A Living Conversation*, pp. 124, 151.

p. 95: "God learns. What God learns…" Carol Gilligan, quoted in Moyers, *Genesis: A Living Conversation*, pp. 153.

Glossary

archaeology—the scientific study of ancient people, their culture, and their civilizations.

artifact—a manmade object, and often one that is to be used for a specific purpose.

covenant—an arrangement between two or more people in which they agree to do certain actions or accept certain obligations or responsibilities.

divinely inspired—something that is influenced by God.

genealogy—the different generations of ancestors that make up a person's "family tree."

geology—the scientific study of the origin, history, and structure of the earth.

gopher wood—the material used to build Noah's ark, according to the account in Genesis; unknown species, but thought to be cypress.

idol—an image in wood, stone, or metal which represents a "god."

laity—nonclergy; not part of the trained ministry.

metaphor—an image or idea that combines two objects that seem dissimilar and shows how they are actually similar. When it is used as an adjective, it refers to a comparison that should not be taken literally.

monotheism—the belief in only one God (*mono* means "one" in Greek).

oral tradition—the transfer of legendary material by word of mouth.

Glossary

patriarchal period—the period of biblical history beginning with Abraham, including his descendants Isaac and Jacob; the list sometimes includes the lineage of Adam through Seth, as well as Moses and Joseph.

polytheism—the belief in many gods (*poly* means "many" in Greek).

primal—having to do with the beginning; from ancient times.

primeval history—Genesis, chapters 1–11; the period of time before the patriarchs. This is mythic-style material, meant to show God's activity in the world from the beginning of the Creation.

prophet—a person who communicates God's word or who speaks through divine inspiration. A woman is called a prophetess.

ruah—a Hebrew word meaning "wind," "breath," or "spirit."

Semitic—the descendants of Noah's son, Shem; used to refer to the Hebrews.

theological—having to do with God or the study of God.

Further Reading

BOOKS FOR YOUNG READERS

Dooley, Tom, and Bill Looney. *The True Story of Noah's Ark* (Green Forest, Ariz.: Master Books, 2003).

Pingry, Patricia A. *The Story of Noah* (Carmel, Calif.: Ideal's Children's Books, 2007).

Poortvliet, Rien. *Noah's Ark* (New York: Harry N. Abrams, 2004).

Singer, Isaac Bashevis. *Why Noah Chose the Dove* (New York: Farrar, Straus & Giroux, 1987).

Spier, Peter. *Noah's Ark* (New York: Picture Yearling, 1992).

BOOKS FOR ADULTS

Bailey, Lloyd. *Noah: The Person and the Story in History and Tradition* (Columbia, S.C.: University of South Carolina Press, 1989).

Cohn, Norman. *Noah's Flood: The Genesis Story in Western Thought* (New Haven, Conn.: Yale University Press, 1999).

Moyers, Bill. *Genesis: A Living Conversation* (New York: Doubleday, 1996).

Ryan, William, and Walter Pitman. *Noah's Flood: The New Scientific Discoveries about the Event That Changed History* (New York: Simon and Schuster, 2000).

Traylor, Ellen Gunderson. *Noah*. (Florence, Ore.: Port Hole Publications, 2001).

Internet Resources

http://sacred-texts.com/index.htm

    This searchable Web site offers the texts of many ancient scriptural and apocryphal documents online. The documents are well indexed. Included are books about religion, mythology, folklore, and more. The sacred texts of the world's great religions can be found here as well.

http://www.muslim.org/english-quran/search/quran-sch.php

    This is an excellent, searchable text of the Qur'an. Searches can be enacted by chapter, verse, and subject matter. The search results are displayed in chart format and are very easy to read.

http://www.talkorigins.org/faqs/flood-myths.html

    This site is a complete anthology of every conceivable flood story around the world, throughout cultures, and across the millennia. The site is organized by world region.

http://www.christiananswers.net/q-abr/abr-a001.html

    Questions about Noah's ark and related questions about Noah and the modern search for the ark are included here. There are some ties to biblical archaeology. The site is in a very readable format.

http://www.arkdiscovery.com/noah's_ark.htm

> This is a representative creationist view Web site. It is sincere in tone and closely aligned with the biblical story. It includes photographs of artifacts and sites purported to be related to the ark. The creationist viewpoint is clearly expressed for people interested in experiencing a complete literal view of Noah's Flood.

http://www.noanswersingenesis.org.au/

> This is a strongly anti-creationist Web site. It confronts the literal view of the Bible from many directions and offers links. It puts the scientific cause in the forefront against those people who hold to the Bible as a scientific text. It is offered here as an opposing Web site to the one above, arkdiscovery.com

http://www.nationalgeographic.com/blacksea/ax/frame.html

> This site concerns itself with a *National Geographic* quest of 1999–2000 to identify an ancient flood which could be the source flood for the large number of ancient flood stories. Their theory is tied to the receding glaciers and Black Sea region. It is a scientific theory investigated with scientific methods.

Index

Aaron, 15
Abraham, 7, 14, 19, 45, 66–67, 74, 80
Adam, 13, 23–26, 34, 42–43, 67, 71, 72
Agri Dagi ("Little Ararat"), 63, 88, 90
agriculture, 32–33, 34, *35*
Ahura Mazda, 57
Akkad, 57–58
Allah, 39, 41, 45, *62*
　See also Islam
Anderson, Bernhard, 69, 72, 88
angels, 27–28, 30, 34
animals, 46–49, 56
　birds, 64–66
　See also ark
Ararat, 63, 88, *89*, 90
archaeology, 18, 20, 91
　and Great Flood evidence, 56–57, 59
　and the search for the ark, 63–64, 88, 90
ark, 11–12
　and the animals, 46–49, 56
　description, 87–88
　Noah builds the, 42–46
　remains of the, 17
　search for the, 63–64, 88, 90
　See also Noah
"arkeologists," 63–64
　See also ark

Armstrong, Karen, 38, 85, 95
Ashurbanipal, 22, 59
Assyrians, 20, *58*, 59
Atrahasis epic, 57, 59
authorship, biblical, 18, 19, *47*, 91
　See also biblical interpretation

Babylonians, 20
Bailey, Lloyd, 90
baptism, 16
　See also Great Flood
Berossus, 59
biblical interpretation, 16–19, 57, 58, 90–95
　literal, 17–18
　scholarly, 18–19, *47*
birds, 64–66
　See also animals
Brueggemann, Walter, 29, 37, 61

Cain and Abel, 26, 67
Cainites, 26–27
Canaan (Ham's son), 75, 81–82, 84–85
Canaanites, 82, 84
Christianity, 11, 13, 15–16
covenant, 6, 70–75, 95, 97
cubits, 43

"The Deluge" (painting), *55*
documentary hypothesis, 18, 19, *47*, 58, 91

Numbers in ***bold italics*** refer to captions.

See also biblical interpretation
doves, 64–65
   See also animals

Ea, 59
Eber (Shem's son), 75
Elijah, 32
Enoch, 13, 14, 27, 29–32, 33–34, 39, 43, 46
Enosh, 27, 36
Eve, 13, 23–26
   See also Adam
evil spirits, 77–79

faith
   and wealth, 7–9
fall of creation, 23–33, 34–37
   and God's promise of destruction, 38–41
Fasold, David, 90
Festival of Weeks, 74
   See also Judaism
Flavius Josephus, 17
floods, ancient, 20, 22, 50–51, 53, 57–60, 91–93
   See also Great Flood
floods, modern, 50, *51*, *52*
folk tales, Jewish. *See* legends, Jewish
form criticism, 92, 93
   See also biblical interpretation

Genesis passages, 16, 17, 40, 93–95
   and the animals on the ark, 46–48, 91
   and Ararat, 63
   ark description, 45
   Cain and Abel, *26*
   creation of the world, 24
   and the end of the flood, 66
   and the fall of creation, 25, *36*
   and the fall of the angels, 28
   God's blessing of Noah, 71
   God's covenant with Noah, 6, 71, 72
   and God's destruction of creation, 38
   and the Great Flood, 53, 54, 57, 61–62

Methuselah's age, 32
Noah's ancestry, 27, 30
Noah's birth, 33
and Noah's birth, 13–14
and Noah's building of the ark, 42–43
Noah's curse on Canaan, 82, **84**
Noah's death, 85
Noah's descendants, 75
Noah's sacrifice, *21*, 67
Noah's vineyard, 80
Noah's wealth, 6
as primeval histories, 20–22
   See also Old Testament passages
Gilgamesh epic, 22, 58, 59–60
Gilligan, Carol, 95
Ginzberg, Louis, 32, 34, 79
Gomorrah, 67
Great Flood, 11, 13, 16, 17, 45, 49, 53–55
   archaeologic evidence of, 56–57, 59
   end of the, 61–63, 64–67
   Enoch's prediction of the, 33
   and God's covenant with Noah, 70–73
   similarities of the, to other floods, 57–60, 91–93
   as worldwide flood, 56–57
   See also floods, ancient
Greenberg, Blu, 62, 70

Haggadah, 24
   See also legends, Jewish
Ham (Noah's son), 39, **41**, 75–76, 79, 81–84, 85
Hebrew Bible, 13
Heschel, Abraham, 40, 42
Hicks, Edward (artist), **48**
historical criticism, 92, 93
   See also biblical interpretation
Hurricane Katrina, 50, *52*

Isaac, 14, 74
Isaiah (book), 74
Ishmael, 14
Islam, 11, 13
   and Allah, 39, 41, 45, **62**

Index 109

and the Qur'an, 14–15, 39, 40–41, 45, 55, *62*

Jacob, 14, 45, 74
Japheth (Noah's son), 39, *41*, 75–76, 79, 81–84, 85
Jared, 27, 28, 36
Jeremiah, 60
Jesus, 15–16
Job, 15
Joktan (Shem's son), 79
Jonah, 15
Joseph, 18
Joshua, 45, 85
Jubilees (book), 45, 54, 67–68, 72, 74, 76–78, 81, 85
  See also Old Testament passages
Judaism, 11, 13, 71, 74
  and the Torah, 19, 24, 76
  See also legends, Jewish

Kenan, 27, 36
Kircher, Athanasius, 87–88
Kish, 20
kosher laws, 71
  See also Judaism

Lamech (Cain's descendant), 27
Lamech (Noah's father), 13–14, 27, 32–33, 39, 40
legends, Jewish, 24, 25–27, 28, 30
  and agriculture, 32, 34, *35*
  and the animals, 49, 56
  birds and Noah, 65
  division of the earth, 75–76
  and evil spirits, 77, 79
  and the Great Flood, 53, 55
  Noah's birth, 33
  Noah's book of wisdom, 42–43
  Noah's invention of tools, 14
  Noah's sacrifice, 67, *68*
  Noah's vineyard, 83
Levi, 45
literary criticism (source criticism), 92, 93
  See also biblical interpretation

Mahalalel, 27, 36

Mastema (demon), 78–79
medicine, 79
"men of renown," 28
  See also angels
Menahem. See Noah
Mesopotamia, 20, 50–51, 53, 57, 60
Metatron. See Enoch
Methuselah, 13–14, 27, 29–30, 32–34
  as prophet, 37, 39–40
Midrash, 24, 25–27, 28
  See also legends, Jewish
Monastery of Saint James, 90
Moses, 19, 45

Naamah (Noah's wife), 39
Navarra, Fernand, 88, 90
Nephilim, 28
  See also angels
Nergal Gate, *78*
New Testament, 6, 7, 9, 40
  See also Old Testament passages
Nimrod (Ham's son), 75, 79
Nineveh, 20, 57, *58*, 75, *78*, 79
Noah
  ancestors of, 13, 27, 29–33, 77
  archaeological evidence of, 20
  and the ark, 11–12, 15–16, 42–49, 87–88
  and birds, 64–66
  birth of, 13–14, 33–34
  book of wisdom of, 42–43, 45
  curse of, on Canaan, 81–82, 84–85
  death of, 85
  descendants of, 39, *41*, 75–79, 81–85
  and evil spirits, 77–79
  God's covenant with, 71–75, 95, 97
  and God's warnings of destruction, 35–37
  and the Great Flood, 53–55, 61–62
  marriage of, 39
  and medicine knowledge, 79
  as prophet, 14–15, 37, 39–42
  sacrifice of, after the flood, *21*, 67–70

110 Noah

spiritual wealth of, 6, 13, 97
and tools, 14
and the vineyard, 6, 14, 80–84
wealth of, 6
and wine, 14, 81
See also ark
Noahide laws, 71–72

offering, Noah's. *See* sacrifice, Noah's post-flood
Old Testament passages, 12, 13, 20, 60, 76, 82–83, 85
and the ark, 45
and evil spirits, 77–78
God's and Noah's covenant, 72, 74
and the Great Flood, 54
Noah and wine, 14, 81
Noah's sacrifice, 67–68
wealth and faith, 7–9
See also Genesis passages
oral tradition, 11, 19, 93

Patterson, David, 29
Paul, 12
Peter, 15–16
Phenech (Japheth's son), 79
population, world, 79
Proverbs (book of), 8

Qur'an
and the Great Flood, 55, *62*
and Noah as prophet, 14–15, 39, 40–41
Noah's building of the ark, 45
See also Islam

racial prejudice, *84*
rainbow, 72–75
See also covenant
Raleigh, Walter, 88
Raphael, 43
Rashi (rabbi), 66
redaction, 92
See also biblical interpretation
reem (animal), 49

sacrifice, Noah's post-flood, *21*, 67–70

Schrof, Joannie M., 94–95
Seth, 26, 27, 29
Shekinah, 27
Sheler, Jeffery L., 94–95
Shem (Noah's son), 39, *41*, 45, 56, 67, 75–76, 79, 81–84
Shemhazai, 34
Shuruppak, 20
Singer, Isaac, 64
Society of Biblical Literature, 93
See also biblical interpretation
Sodom, 67
Solomon, 15, 45
source criticism, 92, 93
See also biblical interpretation
Sumerians, 20, 57, 58–59

Talmud, 24, 32, 34–36, 39, 48, 71, *81*, 83
Tanakh (Jewish Bible), 19, 24
textual analysis, 18, 19
See also biblical interpretation
Theophilus, 17
Titian (artist), *26*
Torah, 19, 24, 76
See also Judaism
Tubal-Cain, 27
Turner, Joseph (artist), *55*

Ur, 20
Utnapishtim, 22, 59–60

Visotzky, Burt, 69

wealth
and faith, 7–9
and the fall of creation, 28
spiritual, 6, 13
Wellhausen, Julius, 90–91
wine, 6, 14, 81, 82
Woods, F. H., 91–92
Wooley, Leonard, 92
Wyatt, Ron, 90

Yima, 57

Ziusudra ("Xiusudra"), 57, 58–59
Zoroastrianism, 57

Illustration Credits

2: Erich Lessing/Art Resource, NY
10: Used under license from Shutterstock, Inc.
12: istockphoto.com/Dale Hogan
15: Used under license from Shutterstock, Inc.
21: © 2008 Jupiterimages Corporation
25: © 2008 Jupiterimages Corporation
26: Cameraphoto Arte, Venice/Art Resource, NY
31: Erich Lessing/Art Resource, NY
35: Used under license from Shutterstock, Inc.
36: National Aeronautics and Space Administration
41: The Jewish Museum, NY/Art Resource, NY
44: HIP/Art Resource, NY
47: Used under license from Shutterstock, Inc.
48: The Philadelphia Museum of Art/Art Resource, NY
51: Deshakalyan Chowdhury/Stringer/AFP/Getty Images
52: PH2 Michael B. Watkins, USN/Department of Defense
55: Clore Collection, Tate Gallery, London/Art Resource, NY
58: Eric Haase/PADIA/Saudi Aramco World
62: Tor Eigeland/PADIA/Saudi Aramco World
63: Kevin Bubriski/PADIA/Saudi Aramco World
65: Werner Forman/Art Resource, NY
68: © 2008 Jupiterimages Corporation
73: Used under license from Shutterstock, Inc.
76: Three Sons of Noah, 12th century (stained glass) by English School (12th century) Canterbury Cathedral, Kent, UK/The Bridgeman Art Library
78: Michael Spencer/PADIA/Saudi Aramco World
81: Used under license from Shutterstock, Inc.
83: Ham mocking Noah by Bernardino Luini (c.1480-1532). Pinacoteca di Brera, Milan, Italy/The Bridgeman Art Library
84: Library of Congress
86: Used under license from Shutterstock, Inc.
87: istockphoto.com/Claudia Dewald
94: © 2008 Jupiterimages Corporation
96: Library of Congress

Cover photo: © 2008 Jupiterimages Corporation

STEPHEN B. WOODRUFF is a 29-year veteran of the elementary school classroom, having taught grades 4 to 6. Mr. Woodruff is also a freelance writer of children's literature and has published several magazine stories and articles. He holds a master's degree in education from SUNY Plattsburgh and attended Princeton Theological Seminary (1977–1978). Mr. Woodruff lives in Morrisonville, New York, with his wife, Jeanette, and his three children, Erik, Rachael, and Andrew.